GHOSTS or DEVILS

PARANORMAL HAUNTING

sandra jeffery

Ghosts or Devils: Paranormal Haunting

Cover image: Kim Akrigg Photography
Model: Nicole Larson

Scripture quotations marked KJV are from the King James Version Bible; Scripture quotations marked RSV are from the Revised Standard Version, copyright 1946, 1952 © 1971, 1973 by the Division of Christian Education of the National Council of the Churches of Christ.

Published by Wheatmark®
1760 East River Road, Suite 145
Tucson, Arizona 85718 USA
www.wheatmark.com

International Standard Book Number: 978-1-60494-541-6
Library of Congress Control Number: 2011937517

Author website: www.sandrajeffery.com

Dedicated to those who are confused and lost
in this world of deception.

"For this purpose the Son of God was manifested,
that he might destroy the works of the devil."
— 1 John 3: 8 KJV

Contents

Acknowledgements

Special Thanks

To my parents for blessing me with a wonderful upbringing; my husband Scott for being a faithful promise keeper and loving partner; and our daughter Deanna for being the sunshine of our lives, a woman of character, and mother to our beautiful grandchild.

Also, thank you to Grace Cooper for mentoring me in the Christian faith and introducing me to Old Testament truths; Denise Sommerville for her thought provoking conversations and insight into the Bible; and my Aunt Shirley Bye-Singh for her professional editing skills and friendship.

And most importantly to God the Father of our Lord Jesus Christ, who without the prompting of His *Holy Spirit's* influence and guidance, this book could not have been written.

Introduction

'Ghosts or Devils, Paranormal Haunting' covers the haunting of homes in particular rather than historical sites and areas of land, and this is because as the author I am writing from my families firsthand experience of living in such a home.

Through this process, I've come to understand that many people in residences deemed as 'haunted' are likely to be stuck in limbo as to what to do about their situation and often out of desperation, many of them have approached the traditional church where the leaders and the congregation have offered prayers for them and their home environment, while others have consulted psychics and mediums looking for answers. Either way it's likely they are still experiencing problems if they haven't moved residences and it is also very likely these unusual manifestations have escalated in their activity. I say this because it seems that once these spirits are acknowledged and are aware of the intention of having them removed, they become even more aggressive in their movements. This is what happened in our experience and judging from what I have read on the subject of haunting, this is a fairly common occurrence within the spirit realm.

Barbara Smith is a well known author of fifteen plus books on ghosts, including *Ghost Stories of Alberta* (the province where our haunting took place), and in her books Barbara tells her readers that these stories are not just passed on to her from third parties but that many of her contributors are people she has met and interviewed in person. She describes them as active, intelligent, and in some cases, very well-known citizens. Out of respect for their willingness to share these profound personal experiences with her, Barbara protects the contributor's anonymity if they request it, which many of them do for good reason.

This anonymity is appreciated because for the most part, any attention gathered from these encounters is usually the worst kind, so it is logical that most people never venture out to share their stories of the paranormal. And when it comes to looking for help through the church to gain assistance, understanding and freedom from this strange phenomenon, many church leaders and members of the church body (with the exception of some Pentecostal or spirit-filled churches) appear to be very fearful about these situations or unlearned in the subject, resulting in some members labeling those experiencing these encounters as having possible psychological problems. Pastors too, for the most part, figure that if they leave the unseen alone, it will leave them alone, so they make no effort themselves to understand or learn about the spirit realm and its workings. And if Pastors aren't making the effort to understand this spiritual phenomenon of haunting, they won't be teaching their congregations about this much needed area of ministry any time soon either.

Unfortunately, for people that are believers in the teachings of the Bible who have been taught that they have authority over the spirit realm through the name of Jesus Christ, when they experience or encounter paranormal activity of this kind in their homes or elsewhere, and don't achieve freedom from it as they believe they should, it often shakes their faith to the core. *"Where is the power and authority in the name of Jesus Christ to cast these spirits out as the scripture tells us?"* They ask. Where do they turn for help and understanding?

For those of you looking for the answers to this perplexing problem of haunting, or are just curious about the subject, here is our haunted house experience along with the steps it took, through many hits and misses, to find freedom from it. I believe that by being put in the situation of living in a haunted home, with no option of moving at the time, this forced us to look for answers that otherwise would not have been found. Here is our story.

GHOSTS
or DEVILS

Background and Subsequent Move to Calgary

November 1994

Before our move to Calgary, Alberta, my husband, daughter and I were living in the city of Grande Prairie, about 400 kilometers north of Alberta's capital city of Edmonton. We were moved to Grande Prairie about five years earlier by the company my husband was employed with, and because we found that we loved the northern part of the province so much, we had hoped to remain there even in our future retirement years.

As many northern Albertans know, it is a paradise for the outdoor type of person because of the surrounding wilderness. There are plenty of lakes to wet a line in and a bountiful supply of moose, elk and deer for the freezer for those who have a taste for wild game. Even the weather is agreeable for the most part, especially in the summer months where the days are longer and the nights are shorter. It's because of these longer days that northerners can grow wonderful vegetable gardens that produce not only the variety of vegetables grown in the region, but more exotic vegetables and fruit such as eggplant and cantaloupe for example. The wilderness is also covered with many kinds of wild berries, including the Saskatoon berry that most prairie dwellers are familiar with. These bushes of berries are literally everywhere, and as a result of this overabundance, Saskatoon pie, jams, jellies and even wine were common food fare for the berry picking sort. It is easy to understand how the north can grow on a person, especially if they enjoy being self-sufficient.

The first four years in Grande Prairie my husband worked his day job and I spent a large part of my time resting and not feeling well overall as a result of having Multiple Sclerosis. Being unemployable because of MS at the time, this closeness to nature helped us to live a lifestyle of frugality out of necessity, and yet while living on one income and a shoe string budget; we still managed to really enjoy life in the process. We even went so far as to heat our city home in winter with firewood that was chopped once, but warmed us twice as we burned it in our wood stove to save on energy costs. There is a lot to be said for the satisfaction that comes with living a life where you can be self-sufficient for a large part of it. It really is a good feeling and fortunately for me, unlike many people with the disease of MS, I was able to remain relatively productive on the home front and able to care for our young daughter at the same time.

However, this ideal lifestyle we were enjoying was to suddenly change for us practically overnight, when my husband was told by the company he worked for, that we were being 'force moved' to Calgary to fill a vacant position there. He'd received the call of his transfer on a Thursday, and was told to report for work the following Monday in Calgary!

After recovering from the shock of this abrupt notice to move, about a month or so later, my husband's company flew me in from Grande Prairie to Calgary to look at several real-estate listings that were picked out for us by our agent for the consideration of purchasing. None of the homes seemed all that appealing to us until we viewed the last residence on the list just prior to my flight back north. We could not believe how nice this house was for the price they were asking, especially after looking at other homes that were close in price but were of no comparison in quality. It had excellent curb appeal and the interior was like that of a new home, immaculate and very well cared for.

The owners of the home were two older ladies, a mother and daughter in their early seventies and nineties, and the reason for selling their house they told us, as we toured it with our real estate agent, was because of the upkeep needed to maintain it. With the daughter caring for her mother along with the house and yard work, they felt that the most reasonable thing for them to do at their age was to move into a retirement village. That sounded pretty logical to us, and we never thought anything about it at the time. We purchased our dream home from them, and moved into it at the end of January, 1995.

After settling into our new home, and not being prone to having an unusual amount of arguments as a couple, we seemed to be at odds with each other on a daily basis. As well, things that once annoyed me personally about certain people and situations years previously I thought I was long past, seemed to re-surface with a vengeance, and I would dwell on these supposed differences or injustices, playing them repeatedly over and over in my mind without resolution. My husband, on the other hand, seemed to take to working in Calgary like a duck takes to a dry creek. Driving in the city was difficult and painful for him with a progressively worsening back injury, and this only seemed to compound his unhappiness with our forced move situation that robbed us of the lifestyle we loved so much.

However, on the bright side there were many perks to moving to Calgary, and one of them was that we were able to enjoy more frequent visits with family who now lived considerably closer. Overall, outside of dwelling on past negatives and arguing with my husband, I was adjusting quite well, getting to know the neighbors and their children, and enjoying the sights in the city along with the close proximity to the mountains and nature of southern Alberta.

Just prior to leaving Grande Prairie, I had experienced a great deal of improvement with my health as a result of seeing a naturopath and following her advice in being proactive with the disease of MS. Through her help, I was able to attend and graduate from Business College that year, and the knowledge I obtained enabled me to produce a self-help newsletter for people with multiple sclerosis shortly after our move to Calgary. I was very excited to have the opportunity to pass on positive health information to other sufferers of this disease, and after settling into our home, I began to write and produce these newsletters and sell them on the Internet to encourage others and help supplement our family income at the same time. As a result, I was on the home front for most of the day, and before long, I began to notice odd things happening around the house.

To begin with, the younger of the two former owners came by the house several times to pick up various items they had left behind when they moved, and when she did, she always shared with me how much they missed their home, neighbors, and even the squirrels that lived in the trees in the back yard. At the time I remember thinking, "Why did you sell the house then?" As far as we knew, they were settling into a retirement village somewhere in the city of Calgary.

About two months later, however, you can imagine how surprised we were when my husband was called by the company he worked for, to put in an order for an installation in a home fairly close to ours that was built by these same two women. This was only about three months after they had sold us their home, and according to my husband, the women's layout of their house was built to the same specifications as ours. These ladies, recognizing my husband, told him that they missed their old house so much that they had one built just like it. I don't know about anyone else, but we found that kind of odd. I know that seniors can regret selling their homes in lieu of living in retirement villages or senior citizen complexes, but all things considered, with the building and finishing of this home completed so soon after selling us theirs, it seemed as though they had this plan in the works for some time. (*We were to find out more details about their lives at a later date that lead us to believe they may have been experiencing this haunting after the death of the daughter's husband who lived there and this may have been why they moved. This is all speculation of course as we never did verify it with them.*)

2

Sensory Manifestation

The first indication that things were not all as they seemed in our home was when a cold presence would envelop me at various times during the day. It would occur often while I was at the sink doing dishes, and almost every night when I went to bed. I would be settled warmly under our bed covers and usually sometime late in the night, I would be awakened suddenly by the feeling of coldness on my face and arms. This sensation would always jolt me awake and I would cling to my husband for comfort and warmth until it passed. I would describe this cold feeling as being like the sensation you would experience if you were being plunged into the minus 40 degree arctic without a coat. Believe me, it was nothing short of a major shock to the system! After experiencing this numerous times, I decided that even though I loved this house, something was there that I couldn't explain and did not want to live with. In desperation, it even crossed my mind at the time to invite the former owners over for tea, in the hopes that whatever was in our home would leave with them.

As well, there were other happenings going on in the house that were unexplainable, such as the times when my husband and I would be together in the living room upstairs, and we would hear the sound of the light switch, operated by a cord in the basement below us, clicking on.

This happened every day at approximately the same time, and yet when we checked in the basement, the light was never on. On one occasion, well into the evening, we thought we heard cupboard doors closing in the kitchen. Thinking it must be our daughter looking for a bedtime snack, my husband checked and found her sound asleep in her bedroom.

While these were just a few of the many strange occurrences experienced by my husband and myself at the time, one incident that stands out in my mind happened one night when I'd worked on my newsletter in the basement where our computer was situated, until about 2:30 – 3:00 a.m. in the morning. After shutting the computer down, and pulling the string on the light switch overhead (the same one that we heard clicking on daily in our living room situated above it), in the darkness I headed for upstairs, humming happily to myself, pleased with what I had accomplished that night with my writing. As I reached the bottom stair in the blackness of the basement, suddenly the computer modem turned back on. It took a pretty forceful push of the button on our modem to start it up, and I cannot describe the sickening feeling that overcame me at the sound of its hum. Something must have pushed it on, and at the very thought of this, terror seemed to overtake me and I wanted to start screaming and running in panic, never stopping and never looking back. It was a paralyzing feeling that I hope to never experience again, and after talking myself through the terror of it and my impulse to become unglued, I forced myself to run over to the computer to shut it off once more. I then made a mad dash up the stairs and into our bedroom where my husband was sleeping. I hurriedly slipped into bed to cling to him all that night; literally scared out of my mind while he slept, oblivious of what had happened. Sleep did not come easily for me after that incident, and needless to say, I never again ventured into the basement to work on our computer late into the night any longer.

While my husband and I never discussed the goings on in our home with each other, outside of exchanging glances when certain antics happened, I made the suggestion to him that I felt we should move. After all, this home was straining our budget, and if we downsized, we could have a better standard of living for it. My husband would disagree with the idea though and argue that he wanted our daughter to grow up in a good, safe neighborhood, and that by selling our home ourselves, rather than through a move with the company, it would eat up the profit and we'd be no better off. Anyway, he reasoned, we might be moving to a smaller center if a job posting he was qualified for came up for bid in the company. I let the subject drop and the fear would subside once more with the busyness of life, until the next incident that is.

Several weeks later, after a morning of working on my newsletter, I had taken a shower and proceeded down the hall to our bedroom with my young daughter and dog tagging along behind me. As I headed over to the night stand to grab my glasses, I tripped over the dozen or so library books I had piled up beside our bed for reading. As I began to restack them, I was suddenly hit with an unbelievably foul stench. Shocked and repulsed by it, I began to frantically look for its source, and while the smell remained for only about 15 seconds, the strength of it was so vile that it had me shaking even after it had dispersed. The only way to describe it would be to say that it smelled of excrement and filth, like the smell of someone who hadn't bathed for a thousand years, never used a toilet, and lived in a garbage dump! I never mentioned the smell to my husband though and the thought of it began to slowly fade from my memory over the course of the day.

One interesting thing about these frightening incidences is that your mind will eventually block them out and you can carry on as usual until something else happens, and then you're back to square one again with the fear. Most people leave these haunted residences as soon as humanly possible, but when you don't have that option, as was in our case, this seems to be how the mind operates to keep you from losing your sanity.

With my husband at work and my daughter at school during the week, I was experiencing these oddities more frequently than either of them, although I kept them to myself at the time. However, I knew we couldn't put off doing something about this presence any longer, when my daughter, out of the blue, asked me if I believed in ghosts. "Of course not," I told her, explaining to her that there was no such thing as a ghost. Then to my surprise, she proceeded to tell me that she believed in them because of the strange things that were going on in our home she had been witnessing and experiencing! She too was aware of this paranormal activity, but not knowing what to say to her about it at the time, I still denied their existence. It was only then that I decided to look for outside help for our situation, in the hopes that we could have this presence removed from our home as quickly as possible.

3

Looking for Answers

I looked in the phone book under psychics and then at our budget, wondering what the cost might be for someone to come through our home and cleanse it or whatever it was that they did, and what my husband would say about this expenditure. Then I thought of the Catholic Church. I had heard that they did exorcisms, which is the removal of demons from people who are apparently possessed by them, and I wondered if they removed spirits from homes through their rituals as well. After calling a local Catholic Church and speaking with a Priest about it, I was told that the church had handled exorcisms at various times, but that it did not handle the cleansing of homes from spirits. They did however, offer the blessing, dedicating and consecrating of homes for believers of the Catholic faith should they request it.

As I continued to look for a possible solution to our problem, I became even more anxious to rid our house of this ghost because of two very unnerving twists to this paranormal activity that happened.

The first of these two incidences took place when my daughter, husband and I decided to head out to the archery club where my husband was a member, to enjoy the peace and quiet of the country side just outside of Calgary. Having the keys to the small, one room building, we let ourselves in to build a fire in the wood burning stove for a wiener roast. My husband, after being unsuccessful in finding matches to get the fire started, suggested I go over to the electric stove in the kitchen to turn on an element so he could get a flame on some newspaper to toss into the stove. However, just as he finished mentioning it, he came across some matches. Soon we had a fire burning and were warming ourselves by it and cooking our lunch at the same time. As we were about to eat our hot dogs, my husband looked over towards the kitchen, and noticed that an element on the stove was glowing red hot. We both headed over to have a look, and with the stove being an ancient model of some sort, it took us a while to figure out how to turn it off. It seemed odd to us that a club member would have accidentally left this element on because there appeared to have been no one at the club house recently as far as we could tell. There were no fresh footprints or tire tracks in the snow outside, and with my husband, daughter and I not venturing near the kitchen until we had noticed the red hot element, how could it possibly have been turned on?

The second incident happened when I was volunteering in my daughters grade three classroom. As I was walking across the room with her teacher, discussing the next step of the assignment we were working on with the students, I was hit by the sickening stench I'd experience in our home some time earlier, and I felt instantly frazzled. Remembering the incident at the archery club and now this, I had a sickening feeling that whatever it was that was in our home was following us, and that we might be dealing with a poltergeist, a spirit or ghost that makes its presence known by incidents that can't be explained. Tell me now, how would you explain that to someone without them believing you are insane? It truly is a terrible place to be in mentally for anyone going through this kind of experience. Famous author, Rudyard Kipling explains the kind of fear that is involved in these situations best in his writing entitled, "My Own True Ghost Story":

"Do you know what fear is? Not ordinary fear of insult, injury or death, but abject, quivering dread of something that you cannot see … and must be felt to be appreciated."

At the school where I worked as a lunch room supervisor, I decided to share with two of my co-workers, in casual conversation about various kinds of strange phenomena, how I thought our home could possibly be haunted. One of the ladies was from England, and because many castles and old buildings are known to be haunted in her native country, she was able to elaborate more on this subject. She told me that these spirits could actually follow you places (I'd already figured this out by our experience, but certainly didn't share that with her), and she also brought me in a video tape the following day of a castle haunting in England. Experts in England apparently rigged up a castle with camera and sound equipment in areas where these ghosts exhibited the most activity, and then they left their machines running overnight when the castle was vacant. It was very eerie watching this tape and seeing things moving and shaking in the dusk, and I wished I'd never taken the tape from her to watch.

When you are going through a haunting yourself, seeing things like this tape only adds to your fear of ghosts. In fact, sometime earlier I'd purchased a book on ghost stories to see if I might find some answers in it on how to rid our home of them, and I found I could not finish the book for that very same reason. It was so unnerving to read of other peoples experiences that were similar and some more terrifying than our own, that I could barely get through even one of the stories without becoming overcome with fright. The fear was so intense that even having the book in our home scared me so badly that I disposed of it in our wood burning stove in our basement. When you don't know what ghosts are all about or how to rid them from your home if it's spooked, reading books on haunting only adds to the fear and confusion.

On top of all this, with my husband being so unhappy at work and myself having to cope with this presence and no option of selling our house and moving, I still felt good about myself until negative thoughts began to pop up in my mind out of the blue. They were so surprising to me that I'd think to myself, "Where did that thought come from? That's not true!" Let me explain that this was not some weird voice I heard, but more what psychologists would call our 'parent tapes', thoughts that run through our heads about ourselves, generally inputted from our parents and life experiences. However, these statements were never spoken to

me or said of me by my parents or anyone else for that matter, nor did I
ever think that way about myself or others, which was why I found them
both odd and amusing at the same time.* The humor of it all fled though,
when an incident happened through an oversight on my part that had
me feeling very bad about myself. It was then that I seemed to embrace
the idea that I just wasn't that good of a person anymore.

An acquaintance in our neighborhood had a daughter the same age
as ours, and she arranged for her daughter to come to our home after
school the following week while she was at work. I've never minded
helping people out when they've needed it, but in this case I was rail-
roaded into doing this favor for her without being asked ahead of time,
and as a result I felt taken advantage of. However, I chose to let it go
but vowed to stand my ground with this woman the next time she tried
overstepping.

We ended up having a surprise visit from some out of town friends
that weekend, and decided we would leave for the mountains with
them until Monday evening. While I made arrangements to cover my
position at the school where I worked, and let the school know of my
daughters planned absence, I totally forgot that this little girl was going
to be coming over to our house after school on Monday. It wasn't until
Tuesday morning that I realized my oversight, and with a sickening
feeling, I promptly called her mother to apologize. According to her
mother, her daughter came to our house after getting off the school bus,
and when no one answered the door, she ran the two blocks to her home
to call her mother, who then promptly left work to be with her. This
woman was a social worker who had witnessed neglect in many forms,
so she understandably was quite angry with me. Fortunately though,
nothing bad had happened, and while she did forgive me for forgetting
and was willing to still be friends, I now seemed to accept these negative
thoughts as truth about myself that I really was a terrible person. I could
not forgive myself for this mistake. As a former block parent, and mother

---

*   see under 'Deliverance Prayer and Healing' about a similar experience.

who has always been overly protective of my child and other children in general, I just can't imagine the anguish some people must go through in situations where the outcome is less favorable. It could, and I'm sure it does, potentially destroy a person.

Lethbridge

1710 14 ave
apr 29. sun?

Dear carol.
I am afraid I am going to
disapoint you very. much. but
I cannot help it. I am sorry
from the bottom of my heart but
we cannot make this trip. I
did figure we could go when
you were here. but since then
some thing has been telling
me not to go, in the first
place. I am not to well
another thing. something seems to
tha ggine me that I should not
go, that that any one said for
me not to go. isn't one word.
I was left on my own what
to do. I want let you kids
take the car. because. I dont
want you to go. dont ask me
why. but thats the way I feel

*Actual letter
written by my
grandmother*

2

and I just cannot shake
it. seems like just feel
strongly. we would be sorry
if I went

pleas dont blam me. I just
cannot help the way I feel
about it. I dont know why
I feel this way but I will
have to do what is best

love from mother

you know I love you and
shirley very much
I hope you find it in your
heart to understand me

and the way I feel.

you will never know much
I hate to tell you this.
but this trip is not for the winter
sorry.

4

The "Angel Series"

It was about this point in time that we received a notice in our mail box about a 'Series on Angels' being put on by a church in our community. As my grandmother was said to have had an 'angel' with her in several photographs taken just prior to her death, I thought it would be interesting to take in this series to find out what insight they might have on the subject. The events that lead up to my grandmother's death were documented in our family history book written by my late aunt, and it described how my grandmother tried to avoid the road trip planned with her two daughters that subsequently lead to her death. On the opposite page is the actual letter written by her to her daughter back in 1962, trying to explain why she wasn't comfortable going on this holiday. Below is a typed version of the letter shown in the photo pages of Prairie Children, Ancestors & Descendants.

> *Dear Carol,*
>
> *I am afraid I am going to disappoint you very much but I can't help it. I am sorry from the bottom of my heart but we cannot make this trip. I did figure we could go when you were here but since then something has been telling me not to go in the first place. I am not too well, another thing something seems to be nagging me that I should*

not go, not that anyone said for not to go. Not one word. I was left on
my own what to do. I won't let you kids take the car because I don't
want you to go, don't ask me why but that's the way I feel and I just
can't shake it, seems like just feel so strongly we would be sorry if we
went. Please don't blame me I cannot help the way I feel about it. I
don't know why I feel this way but I will have to do what is best.

Love from Mother

You know I love you and Shirley very much. I hope you find it in
your heart to understand me and the way I feel. You will never know
how much I hate to tell you this but this trip is not for this winter.
Sorry.

A short while later, my grandmother wrote the girls that she had
changed her mind and decided she would go with them, and whatever
was to happen, would happen. It was on this trip that she was killed in a
car accident that her two daughters walked away from. Below my Aunt
Shirley writes of the experience:

"It was the most horrible experience but I was young and worked very
hard at trying to work through the grief and trying not to let her death be in
vain – that being, to try to appreciate people and appreciate the moment. I
denied guilt because mom had had two premonitions. 1. That she should not
travel and 2. She might as well travel because it was going to happen anyway.
Today, my heart feels heavy when I write about it. It is essential to live in
today."

Understandably, my curiosity was peaked when this opportunity
came to attend the 'Series on Angels' and through this series I soon
learned that angels, according to the Bible, delight in the death of God's
saints. My grandmother was a Christian woman, and if this was her
appointed time, maybe this mist in the photos was actually an angel
watching over her. Then again, I'm more inclined to think it could just
be the film, but with her having the premonition she did, was it an angel
with her, knowing her end was near?

What I also learned about angels that was disturbing for me, was
that not all supernatural forces are good and not all angels are from

God. This is why we are told not to call upon them for help, guidance or whatever. If we are going to have an angel, it will be issued to us by God alone. We are not to beckon them as many people are now doing today.

"And when I heard and saw them, I fell down to worship at the feet of the angel who showed them to me; but he said to me, "You must not do that! I am a fellow servant with you and your brethren the prophets, and with those who keep the words of this book. Worship God." — Revelation 22: 8, 9 RSV

"Let no man beguile you of your reward in a voluntary humility and worshipping of angels, intruding into those things which he hath not seen, vainly puffed up by his fleshly mind." — Colossians 2: 18 KJV

With the knowledge gained over a number of weeks, I began to realize that maybe this haunting presence in our home wasn't the spirit of the former owner's husband causing problems (as mentioned earlier, we'd learned he had died two years prior to the selling of her house), but it was the workings of the devil to have us think so. What we were dealing with was an angel of the devil himself, and not some poltergeist or ghost from a past life walking the floor as we had previously thought.

Towards the end of the Series on Angels, a woman stood up to the podium and related an experience that she had had with her son that involved an evil spirit, and how the Lord Jesus Christ, through continual prayer and quoting of scripture for numerous hours, had delivered them of its presence. Hearing her testimony, I felt I could approach this church for help with our haunting problem, as it appeared they seemed open to the supernatural and understood its workings. I opened up to a member of the church about our situation, and she took it upon herself to arrange for one of the pastors to accompany her through our house to cleanse it.

Several days later they came by, and we discussed our situation and decided we would gather around our living room table to pray together before proceeding with a walk through of the house. Suddenly, just as we began praying, our dog began to act rather peculiar. She had gotten hold of some Lego (toy building blocks) of my daughters, and ran under the table we were praying around. She then proceeded to chew so loudly on them that it was hard to concentrate or to hear each other pray. Then she tried other distractions, such as chewing the minister's shoes that he'd left at the front door when he came in. Then, when we began the home cleansing, she proceeded to tear after us like a race horse as we walked through the house. Trying our best to ignore her, we prayed together in each of the rooms, and in the specific areas where there appeared to have been paranormal activity, the Pastor commanded the spirit or spirits to leave in the name of the Lord Jesus.

After this ritual of sorts was performed throughout the entire house, I felt a wonderful sense of peace as did our dog who went back to sleeping on the couch. However, this peace was short lived when the minister upon leaving, told me that we still might continue to have a problem with this spirit or spirits, and that our haunting may not be quite over for us just yet! What he meant by that statement, I wasn't sure and felt very troubled by it. As time began to pass though, the presence appeared to be gone completely. There was no further activity after the walk through and as a result, with my faith in a living God strengthened, I began to attend church on a regular basis, becoming a member of a weekly Bible study group and growing spiritually.

5

Charmer

Just prior to my incident of receiving negative thoughts about myself, I'd made friends with a neighbor who was seeking help for a medical condition, and was a patient of a doctor that practiced hypnotherapy for the treatment of disease. She had spoken with me several times about how good this doctor was, and suggested I see him for help with my MS. While I thought the theory of treating disease with hypnotherapy was interesting, I had no desire to make an appointment to see him, seeing as I had my MS under control as it was. However, I gave it a second thought when I adopted this negative thinking pattern. As I became desperate to lose the negativity I'd picked up, I decided to go for treatment in the hopes of finding relief from it, and if improvement in my MS happened along with it, that would be a bonus too! My negativity however, was what concerned me most at the time.

As it was, I ended up seeing this doctor about 6 to 7 times, and each week he would tape our sessions, and I would take these tapes home to listen to them daily until our next visit. I found that these tapes seemed to work somewhat with the negativity, but nothing noticeably with my MS. However, I was certain that if I listened to them daily as the doctor recommended, I would not only be free of the negative thoughts, but also possibly of my MS.

Having attended church on a regular basis for some time now, and practicing daily devotions that involves scripture reading and prayer, one morning in particular, I couldn't decide if I should listen to my hypnosis tape or do my devotions first. It was becoming a tossup as to which one to start with each morning, but this particular day I decided on beginning with my devotions. In the process of praying, I proceeded to tell God about my need for these hypnosis tapes because He hadn't healed me of my MS or my negative thinking, so I was sure that He would not have any problem with me listening to them. After all, I reasoned, there are many path ways to healing and maybe this was the one that was right for me.

That being said, I did ask God to *go before me* to listen to these tapes in my closing prayer. At the time I didn't know that scripture points out that the God of the Bible is a jealous God, and that hypnosis is defined under the term *'charmer'*, and is considered an occult practice and an abomination to God. What happened next seemed to confirm the following scriptures to me:

"For you shall worship no other god, for the Lord, whose name is Jealous, is a jealous God." – Exodus 34: 14 RSV

"For I the Lord your God am a jealous God" — Exodus 20: 5 RSV

I went to our bedroom, closed the curtains and got into my usual position of laying down comfortably on our bed with a pillow propped behind my head, and in this relaxed state, I turned on the tape recorder that was situated on the night table, closed my eyes, and waited for the doctors words to put me under. Well, I waited, and waited, and waited, but his words did not come.

After fast-forwarding the tape and stopping it to hear nothing but the same sound of silence, I rewound it back to the beginning and pressed play again, only to be met by the sound of dead air once more. Frustrated, I stopped the tape recorder and opened it up to find the tape unraveled and useless. Surprised, I decided then and there that these hypnosis tapes must not be right with God, and I quickly disposed of them.

"There shall not be found among you any one who burns his son or his

daughter as an offering, anyone who practices divination, a soothsayer, or an augur, or a sorcerer, or a charmer, or a medium, or a wizard, or a necromancer. For whoever does these things is an abomination to the Lord; and because of these abominable practices the Lord your God is driving them out before you. You shall be blameless before the Lord." — Deuteronomy 18:10 – 14 RSV

"The Lord your God who goes before you will Himself fight for you." — *Deuteronomy 1: 30 RSV*

I shared what happened with my hypnosis tape in a small church study group I was a part of, and another woman in the group shared the story of what happened to her mother that involved hypnosis as well. Her mother it seems had been trying to quit smoking, and at the recommendation of her pastor she went to see a Christian doctor who practiced it. What she found out from this doctor was that he had discontinued using hypnosis for treatment sometime earlier when the last client he hypnotized ended up sliding off the reclining chair onto the floor, and slithered around like a snake with his eyes bugging out. The doctor claimed he looked like a serpent! (Maybe the doctor had asked God to go before him that particular day too?)

6

———

Fasting for Clarity

At this point in time, my husband did not attend church with me and it was like pulling teeth to get my daughter to go. He knew that the minister and believer had come through our home to cleanse it (we never shared this with my daughter until a much later date), and he was quite happy about the outcome but still had no desire to attend church on Sunday, especially since he was working 10 day stretches and had only every second Sunday off. He needed his sleep he reasoned, and more often than not, I allowed our daughter to stay home with him so they could spend time together, making pancakes and catching up on the week's activities.

Still troubled in the back of my mind that this spirit may or may not still be present in our home because of what the pastor said previously, just prior to Christmas in 1998, I took it upon myself to fast to see if there was still any cause for concern, and if so, that it would be revealed to me.* I'd read the following scripture in the Bible that tells us the purpose of fasting, and being prompted by it, I decided to fast for three days.

———

* read under 'Deliverance Prayer and Healing' chapter about my error in doing this.

"Is not this the fast that I have chosen? To loose the bands of wickedness, to undo the heavy burdens, and to let the oppressed go free, and that ye break every yoke?" — Isaiah 58: 6 KJV

Things seemed fine the first day of the fast, until late into the night when I was awakened by the abrupt pushing down of my left leg from its usual bent knee position.

In the depths of sleep, I half awoke, thinking that I must be irritating my husband sleeping like this with my knee bent and next to his back, and while it never seemed to bother him before, maybe it was bothering him now? I was in such a deep state of slumber that even when I opened my eyes and didn't see him beside me, I still fell immediately back to sleep. Several hours later in the early morning though, I was awakened again by the abrupt pushing down of my left leg from its bent position, only this time it jolted me wide awake! My husband, to my horror, was not even in the bed with me. Terrified, I jumped up and ran from our bedroom and through the house looking for him, finally finding him asleep in our downstairs bedroom. When I awoke him to tell him what had just happened, he told me that he wasn't in our bed at all that night because when he went to turn in, he noticed I was crowding the bed and decided he'd sleep downstairs rather than disturb me. With a sickening feeling overcoming us, we realized our problem was still in our home and was not going to go away easily. Fortunately for me though, this was the first and last time I experienced anything of a physical nature by this 'spirit'. *(This physical pushing is actually a fairly common occurrence that happens to residents when they become pro-active in attempting to rid their homes of the demonic, as read about in numerous books on the subject.)*

Not deterred, I continued my fast, adamant that this spirit was not going to persist in our home. Once more I was overly anxious and especially concerned about the welfare of our daughter. I continued with my daily devotions, attending church and Bible study, but I began to wonder what I was doing wrong in my Christian walk that this problem was still not resolved. Wasn't the name of the Lord Jesus Christ all powerful?

Previously to the first time the pastor and believer came through our home, I'd been able to smell that horrible stench I'd described earlier at certain times and in various places, while my husband appeared not to experience it. Sure enough though, three days after my fast, my husband was home sick from work for what lasted a week, and during his time on the home front, he too began to smell that vile stench. Fortunately for me, I could no longer smell it, and it seemed that while I was now free from the workings of this spirit, my husband and daughter unfortunately were not.

What became even more disturbing for me was the start of my daughter's strange behavior. I would catch her sitting in our living room on the carpet wrapped in a blanket and seeming very sad. When I would ask her why she was so sad, she would say it was because she wanted to go home. I'd ask her what she meant by that because she was home. Did she miss our home up north I wondered? She couldn't seem to tell me where this home was. After this happened numerous times over a two week period, I finally got upset with her and told her I'd had enough of her silly talk, and I didn't want to hear her talk foolishness like that again. I was both agitated by it and frightened at the same time. This strange behavior did not make any sense to me—that was until a young lady with a 'bad angel' came to our church looking for help.

7

The "Bad" Angel

"Satan himself masquerades as an angel of light."
— *2 Corinthians 11: 14 KJV*

Shortly after these incidents with my husband and daughter, the believer that was leading our small group called me about a young girl who had come to our church looking for help. What had happened to her was, on the advice of her psychic friend, she had gotten in touch with her 'angels', and unfortunately she had beckoned to herself a 'bad angel' as she called it. This angel was tormenting her and she wanted help in ridding herself of its presence, and she had been referred to our church by a woman working at an angel store in the city that had heard of our 'Series on Angels'. Because the youth pastor did not want to counsel this young girl on his own for ethical reasons, I agreed to meet with him and the elder believer (the same woman who came with the pastor to cleanse our home), to see how we could be of help to her.

We met at the church the following day, and this young girl told us what this angel was doing and telling her about herself that wasn't true and how she was particularly harassed at night by it, so much so that she couldn't sleep even with the light on. After spending some time with her, the pastor, because of time constraints, asked us if we would be willing to work with her on our own, and we agreed with the young

girl to meet the next day at the elder's home where we would continue
our counseling.

Because of our home situation still being unresolved at that time,
I expressed my concern to the elder that it would be a false witness for
me to try and help someone with this kind of problem. How could I be
of help to someone experiencing demonic problems, when our family
wasn't free of demonic activity either? She suggested that I needed to
keep in mind the source of this spirit (the devil) and to help out anyway,
which I then hesitantly agreed to do.

I arrived at her home early the next day, and we discussed what
approach to take before the girl arrived, and we decided it would be a
good idea for her to do the *12 Steps to Spiritual Freedom* outlined in *The
Bondage Breaker* written by Neil T. Anderson. When she came by later,
we sat at the kitchen table and discussed these steps with her. She told
us she had done them already so we asked her if she had prayed and
confessed everything about her past to God. She told us that some of
her past sins she hadn't confessed, and then she proceeded to change
the subject to tell us what this spirit or angel was saying to her right at
that very moment that was demeaning. When I made light of what this
spirit was saying to her, she said to me, "Do you know what it is telling
me right now?" "What's that?" I asked. "It's telling me, 'I want to go
home,'" she said. Right away I could feel the hair on my arms stand on
end, and I realized that I was dealing with something I knew nothing
about, and that it was stronger than anything I was prepared to deal
with. What this spirit had said was the same thing that my daughter
was saying when she was wrapped in the blanket in our living room and
looking sad.

After driving this young girl to her bus stop a short time later, when I
returned home I called the elder and told her I would not work with this
girl under any circumstances, and that this was something she would
have to take on herself to do with one of the pastors from the church.
She understood my position because of the situation with our daughter,
and she did continue to work with this girl on several other occasions,
but found that she was not willing to change her life or to accept the Lord

Jesus as her personal savior with any serious commitment involved. The last I heard about this situation, the girl was doing somewhat better with her 'bad angel' problem after moving out to eastern Canada to be with friends.

8

Time to Move House

When I got home that evening, I discussed what had happened at our meeting with my husband, and we both came to the agreement that we were moving out of our home as soon as possible. I phoned our youth pastor from the church and told him of our situation and what had happened with this girl, and shared with him our plans for moving.

Our pastor suggested I do the *12 Steps to Spiritual Freedom* by Neil Anderson as well that same day, and the next morning he asked the ladies at the Friday morning prayer meeting to pray for us. I did the 12 steps outlined in the book and received some comfort from it, all the while hoping that by doing them, our problems would be over once and for all.

Sunday rolled around and we attended church with some friends that day, and my husband noticed our name was under the 'Prayer Column' in the church bulletin, but didn't mention it to me until later that evening. *(This was obviously a God incidence because names placed under the 'prayer column' are picked from attendants names by alphabetical listing, and the first letter of our last name just happened to be for that day.)*

We had a good day visiting with company and that night, after preparing for bed before retiring, I began to read scripture while my husband talked long distance to a friend in our living room just outside of our bedroom door. Just as I was closing the Bible to call it a day, and was reaching over to turn the light out on the night table, I suddenly felt that cold chilling presence I'd experienced in the past envelop me. To say that I was surprised and shocked would have been an understatement! After all that we had been through, it was still in our home? I was so angry I wanted to scream out loud at it to *get out*, but with my husband on the telephone so close by, I restrained myself and whispered, "Satan, you have no business being here. Get out of here in the name of Jesus!"

Just as I finished speaking the words, I heard the sound of what visually would have been a herd of animals of some kind, running and crashing from my side of the bed, through our computer room next to us, through our daughter's room, and out the back of the house. The sound of it was so loud and disruptive that my husband told his buddy he was talking with, "Hold on a minute! Something's going on here!" and he dropped the phone and ran down the hall looking for what had made the huge ruckus. After searching and checking the entire house upstairs and down for the source of the commotion, he headed back to the phone to tell his friend that he couldn't figure out what had made all the noise. In awe of what had just transpired, I decided to tell him the next morning about it, and his only response to it was to say, "Now, I really want to move…!"

9

Time to Move Churches

Now confident that our home was unoccupied by demons with no more smells or episodes with my daughter wanting to go home, etc., surprisingly to me, I still had my negative thoughts. I believe this was partly due to being told numerous times by a member of the church, after I shared with her how I wished I had never mentioned my haunted house story with anyone because of the fear I was being judged, that the church was a *very forgiving* church. In effect, my interpretation of this statement was that the church was judging me and obviously didn't take what I had to say seriously. This caused me to have hard feelings towards the pastors, elders, and whoever else I assumed might be judging me, believing them to be lacking spiritually that they would leave me in the hands of someone inexperienced in spiritual warfare and secondly, that they would judge me for having shared my experience. This shook my self-confidence to the core. On one hand I was told I was believed, and yet on the other hand, I was told I wasn't! (*When I confronted this woman at a later date to ask what she meant by the church being very forgiving, she had no recollection of even saying it.*)

For this reason alone I intended to leave the church, and was in the process of looking for another denomination to attend, when a church member and I had the opportunity to go to a service at an extension church of our own denomination that had a guest pastor speaking who was profiled in one of the *Transformation* videos that many Christians have seen. For those who haven't seen these videos, they are about entire communities that have been transformed through repentance, corporate prayer, and the claiming of God's word over their land with miraculous results.

After getting seated, and listening to the music and introductions, this particular pastor from California got up to speak, and during his sermon he began to talk about the importance of remaining in the church we were at. Turning to focus his attention to the area where I was seated in the audience, he made eye contact with me as he began to explain the reasons why. It was like having my own personal sermon on the subject and this was more than a little odd, seeing as there was close to seven hundred-plus people in attendance that evening. Because my friend knew of my intention to leave our church, she thought this was very funny. On the other hand, I didn't find it amusing at all and I was very upset about it in fact. However, it was because of this talking to by this pastor from the pulpit that night, that I remained at our church for several more years until our move from Calgary, still feeling judged by who knows who, but growing spiritually in many areas in the process.

10

Lifting of Oppression

This was not the end of our house story though. After being free from any activity in our home and living at peace for a number of years, my daughter still described our house as having a black cloud over it when she came home from school each day. I figured there wasn't anything happening in our home to make her feel that way, except maybe some negativity possibly because of all that had happened to my husband and I that wasn't totally forgiven. My husband had been in an ongoing litigation with a company he'd worked for that treated him unjustly after he sustained a serious back injury while working for them, and it had been many years of trying to have this injustice resolved that was very hard on us both financially and emotionally. After reading Isaiah 58: 6 on fasting again, I noticed it mentioned the word oppression, so I took it upon myself to look the word up in several dictionaries. The definition of oppression is as follows:

"Unjust or cruel exercise of authority or power as well as a sense of being weighted down in body or mind, to burden spiritually or mentally and to weigh heavily upon, to suppress or depress."

Both my husband and I decided we should fast together for this oppression to lift, and when the day of fasting was through, I also attended a prayer meeting that evening for more prayer support. Afterwards, what was surprising to us was that the black cloud that left wasn't work related, but appeared to be in the atmosphere of our home. It was very evident by the same evening that something oppressive was gone from our household. About two weeks later our daughter (we hadn't told her about us fasting about the oppression yet either), complained that she was having trouble coping with things being so positive on the home front. It was a good thing, she acknowledged, but it was just that she wasn't used to it after all those years, and she was having a hard time adjusting to it!

I believe this was the missing piece in all of this spiritual warfare, and that is the critical importance of fasting and prayer in these situations. The Lord Jesus Christ himself told his disciples that some of these demons can only be removed through prayer and fasting. *"But this kind does not go out except by prayer and fasting." — Matthew 17: 21 KJV*

11

"Trust Me"

While living with various adversity daily back then for a number of reasons, financial being a large part of it, we still tithed to our church even though technically we could not afford it. *(I'll explain why this is important further into this chapter.)* I made a habit of walking our dog every morning and one day I was so fed up with what was happening to us, that I decided to walk our dog twice so I could have a walk/talk with God about our circumstances and frustrations.

As I walked, I reminded God (to myself of course), that I did not ask to be placed in a haunted house, nor did I appreciate being placed in a church unfamiliar with the spiritual realm, resulting in the very long process it took to have the demonic removed from our home, and my having to tolerate judgmental attitudes I'd received from certain church members about our experience. On top of that, I had taken two full-time jobs over a two year period with a school board that I had told God specifically I would not work for because of the stress involved and my current health condition of MS. Yet because these jobs lined up with God's will for me that couldn't be denied due to the circumstances leading up to them, in the process of working, I'd lost some vision in my right eye due to a related MS condition called optic neuritis. (It has since cleared up 100%.)

Surprisingly, I had had a nagging feeling for several years prior to working for the school board that I was to do something that pertained to feeding people, so I volunteered with our church's food bank thinking it would go away, and yet somehow I knew this was not what the nagging feeling was about. However, by being obedient in taking the two jobs I didn't want initially, after observing and being a part of the first schools "feed the students" program, I was able to bring the idea forward to the next school I worked at that didn't have this much needed program in place. A good friend and her husband supplied the first $1,000.00 to get it up and running, and from there it was taken over by her church whose members partner-shipped with the school to finance it. It was only then that the nagging feeling left me, so I knew this had been God's leading. However, I complained to God, "Did I have to lose more of my health in the process?"

Along with my husband and I both having serious health problems over the years with no family members living near us to fall back on for emotional or financial support, our finances dwindled fast, and I was furious that we had been in a long arbitration with the company my husband had worked for that had dismissed him after his injury. The arbitrator, while promising to get the decision made in our favor or in the companies favor within three months after the arbitration, had stretched his decision time on to six plus months, leaving us in limbo as to what we should be doing – moving or staying in Calgary. It didn't help to hear that another arbitrator with this same company didn't make a decision in a year's time in another injury case, which meant the arbitration process had to start all over again. This is very cruel to do to an injured worker as by that time they likely would have lost everything, including their sanity.

Now, on top of this, while it was a God send that my husband had gotten a job in another city that wasn't further aggravating his injury, it resulted in us being separated as a family for about a year. Disheartened, lonely, and discouraged, after pouring out all of my hurt, anger, and frustration to God, I simply asked, "What do I do with all of that?"

At that precise moment, I was walking past a row of cars and as I looked to my left, to my surprise, written on the top of the back window of a small burgundy car, were the words, *Trust Me*! At first I thought to myself, "Who in the world would put that on the back windshield of their vehicle?" As I continued walking past the car to the end of the street, I realized those words were for me! I circled the block and came back to look a second time at the car to see if I was seeing things, and sure enough, the words were still there and as bold as ever in large white letters in script. Rather than just tell my family about it and have them wondering about me, because my husband was out of town, I took my daughter over to see the letters on the car to verify I wasn't seeing things.

A month or so later, we received our arbitration decision after I had attended a healing retreat given through *Ellel Ministries.* This ministry was critical for me to have prior to our move, or I would still be struggling with certain issues in my life today that would not have been resolved otherwise.

It's true that God speaks to all of us individually in various ways, and as a result of this I constantly remind myself to put my trust in Him as He has the big picture in mind that is to materialize. This has helped me to continue carrying on, and as a result, we are now starting to see wonderful blessings in our lives.

What is exciting about God's promises is that if we do the requirements, He fulfills them over time. Understanding the importance of tithing for example, because we were good stewards of what little money we had, tithing since coming to Christ, and putting aside RRSP's (registered retirement savings plan monies) even when we couldn't afford to, when we were several weeks from losing our home and the stock market was at an all time low, suddenly one of our stocks went sky high and we took this opportunity to cash it in to the tune of a profit of $12,000.00. This stock was high for only two days before it dropped again, and because we had no one to bail us out of our predicament financially, we believe God took the reins in this area and we were so thankful for it! However, if we had not been good stewards of tithing and managing our finances even though we were struggling terribly, I don't believe this would have happened.

Another example of how God can work in this area of finances too, was when we heard of a family we knew that was in dire straits financially, so we gave them $100.00 anonymously out of our budget for our monthly power, phone and utilities bills. These bills were approximately $300.00 a month at the time, and yet when our bills came in, they totaled only $200.00! The family was blessed by our giving and we were blessed to see God's hand move in the keeping of His promises.

"He who is kind to the poor lends to the Lord, and he will repay him for his deed." — Proverbs 19: 17 RSV

Currently we are now in a nice home that we can afford, and my husband has a job that suites him physically in helping his injury, which is no small feat seeing as there is less that 10% of men who have been injured to the extent of my husband, that obtain gainful employment in their lifetime. We are blessed financially where we can make ends meet and I no longer lose sleep over our money problems as I had for many, many years.

"Bring the whole tithe into the storehouse, so that there may be food in My house, and test Me now in this,' says the Lord of hosts, 'if I will not open for you the windows of heaven and pour out for you a blessing until it over-flows." — Malachi 3:10 KJV

And to top this all off, the timing was perfect for the selling of our former home and moving to our new home back in 2005. *Our mortgage was up for renewal on February 1st, 2005 and our house sold with the pos-session date of February 1st, 2005.* This meant we had no payout penalty at the bank, and what was even more amazing was that the purchaser of our home asked us for an earlier possession date of January 24th. We were also able to take possession of our new home on January 24th, and in the process of moving, we found the 'purple page' that was issued at church the Sunday of our house cleansing, and it was January 24th, six years earlier! At the time I was using a daily devotional book entitled *Experiencing God*, written by Henry Blackaby, and on January 24th, it read as follows: *"They said to Him, 'Rabbi, where are you staying?' He said to them, 'Come and see.' They came and saw where he was staying, and remained with Him that day."* — *John 1: 38 – 39 KJV.* To me this meant that we had moved from our possessed home in Calgary, to a home that is in God's possession in that He is with us and we are in Him, as is Jesus with all believers.

12

The Background on
Our Former Home

From what we were able to gather from neighbors in conversation, the daughter's husband of the house had died from emphysema about two years before we bought it. They appeared not to be very friendly from what we were told (maybe this was the man only – I'm not sure), and if children were playing outside and their ball accidentally crossed over into their yard, all noise would stop on the street as fear set in as to who would be the one to retrieve it, probably out of the fear of being scolded. The couple also seemed to have an intense hate for one another, and when the man died, his wife donated his body to science at the university, where he was pickled for a year, as one of our neighbors described it. This same neighbor went on to say that as far as he was concerned, that was the best place for him! He knew him to talk to and said that he felt this man was truly evil by the conversations they had and the things he had said. He also told us this man believed that the world was a terrible place and that everyone in it was terrible. *(Could that have been why I picked up such negativity? Who knows?)* Needless to say, while I'm sure they had their redeeming qualities; they weren't exactly endearing people in the neighborhood.

When we shared with a neighbor and his wife some of the incidents that happened in the house, they believed for certain that it was being haunted by this man. In their attempt to be helpful, through their church of spirituality they attended, they offered us the services of one of their mediums to come through our home to check it out for us. We shared with them our experience of having our home cleansed, but this well-meaning couple still insisted on calling us several times to offer their help. They could not grasp the idea that the house was actually cleansed of this 'spirit', and while they understood the power of the name of Jesus, they also believed that Jesus was only one of many pathways to God. They believed in Jesus and the Bible they told us, but also in life after death for everyone, regardless of how they lived their lives. Like many of us, by not reading our Bibles and yet professing to believe in Jesus Christ, we miss what scripture tells us about death, along with what it warns us to look out for. Because of this, we are often unaware of what we are doing or practicing that may be anti-scriptural and potentially dangerous for us, and those around us. (*Like myself with the hypnosis tapes.*)

"*But Jesus answered and said to them, 'You are mistaken, not under-standing the Scriptures nor the power of God."* — *Matthew 22: 29 KJV*

"*For as yet, they did not understand the Scripture."* — *John 20: 9 KJV*

13

What I Have Learned about "Haunting"

With regard to the possession and oppression areas of the supernatural, from what I have learned and read about on this subject, possessions and oppressions are not usually prayed over and then disappear as many Christians seem to think they should. People in general don't get prayed for and have their problems suddenly resolved, and this is because for the most part healing is a process. When healing doesn't happen for us, it can often be because of un-forgiveness on our part, pride, un-confessed sin and un-repentance, dabbling in the occult, idol worship, etc.

A good example of this is our house haunting. If it had been resolved quickly, I wouldn't be as committed to my belief in Jesus Christ as I am, and I certainly wouldn't have written this book on the subject. Or, with regard to my negative thinking, if I would have shared my problem with other believers and been prayed over for deliverance, I might have been healed instantly of it, or at least a lot sooner than I was. In hindsight, it would also have been wise to have a cloak of prayer over me in the writing of this book, as many Christian authors warn that a *prayer covering* is necessary for those investigating and exposing the demonic so that they don't become influenced by these spirits, and possibly be oppressed or possessed by them in the process.

(One of our youth pastors from our former church decided to preach on 'witchcraft' a number of years ago, and told the elders afterwards that the week of preparation for his sermon was the worst week of his life. In the search for material on the subject to put his sermon together, he claimed he experienced a loss of self-confidence and became very scattered in his thoughts and actions. When he preached that Sunday on the occult, he would stop frequently in mid-sentence after losing his train of thought, and this was something that had never happened to him before or since that time. His conclusion at the end of his sermon was for Christians to avoid the occult, and to stay away from investigating it altogether. 'Don't go there' was his message.)

14

What to Do If We Are in a "Haunted" House

There could be any number of reasons why our home may have been opened up to the invasion of the demonic. There may have been a curse put against the land our home was built on, previous residents or homeowners may have been dabbling in the occult, or there may have been a murder or some kind of abuse that happened on the premises. A haunting can also result from having a home built on a sacred site of our North American Indians for example, and this theory matches up with another family's experience we were acquainted with, that lived in the same area as us in Calgary. Their experience was different than ours in that they had constant native drumming and chanting in one of their children's bedrooms, and the movements of a poltergeist in their home that opened curtains and did other odd things. Land can be cursed as well as people, and these curses often affect those whose homes are built on these sites if their circumstances warrant it or not.

It should be stressed as well, that a person's characteristics and personality that may have lived or died in a particular area or home can convincingly be projected by spirits. It is thought by some that these are spirits that have come back to finish unresolved issues they may have had in their past life (as we thought too initially), or a person could be living in an area that principalities and demonic powers govern over as the Bible points out. In secular books on haunting, they mention that in various cities around the world there are continuing problems of the paranormal in certain city blocks and areas that are constant and consistent, remaining throughout time. This matches up with the governing areas of demonic powers the Bible speaks of in the following chapter in the book of Ephesians.

"For we wrestle not against flesh and blood, but against principalities, against powers, against the rulers of the darkness of this world, against spiritual wickedness in high places."
— *Ephesians 6: 12 KJV*

Why I believe our 'Problem' resurfaced

First of all, I should never have fasted to ask God if the demonic was still in our home when there was no evidence of it. This is because the spirit realm is always around us, and I was basically giving it permission to resurface. Of course I did this because of the doubt that was put in my mind when I was told our situation might not be resolved that easily. Yet looking back, I can understand why the Pastor made that statement, and it is because there are many who are not really committed in their belief in Jesus Christ and walking according to His Word, who inadvertently leave an open door to the demons to once again surface.

Another reason why a person may have continual problems with the spiritual realm is the result of un-repentance. I'd read about a Christian woman who lived in a haunted home where the spirits could not be removed, and when she repented of the habit of stealing she'd carried with her since her youth, she had no further problems. When we practice things that are contrary to the Bible's teachings, we can be asking for all kinds of trouble, and for some it can unknowingly result in us giving authority to the demonic to be present in our lives.

In our circumstance, I believe the demons in our place of residence left the second time around because of corporate prayer offered through the church body, and by my speaking out loud the name of the Lord Jesus Christ to cast them out.

"And these signs shall follow them that believe; In my name they shall cast out devils." — Mark 16: 17 KJV

The overhanging oppression of our home was removed by fasting and praying, so possibly these demons were more difficult to remove than others.

If you are in the situation of living in a haunted residence, first of all, talk with your pastor about it in confidence, and if he cannot help you, ask him to refer you to someone who understands spiritual warfare and is experienced with it. God willing this book has given some clarity and direction as to what is needed to be done to obtain freedom from this spiritual oppression.

15

---✦---

"Warning, Warning, Warning"

While it has been unnerving mentally for me to be writing and documenting about the demonic for seven-plus years without a prayer covering, mostly due to my reluctance to keep asking for prayer, it's been a good thing as I've learned even more about spiritual warfare over time. This is because the Holy Spirit has been revealing more and more of the truths in the Bible and what we are to be aware of. I'd like to share with you now, what happened when I brought several books into our home that the Bible would classify as abominable. This is a good reminder that when we disobey what the scripture teaches, the paranormal can regain access into our homes and lives through assumptions we often make as Christians.

A friend and I decided a few years ago that we would try out different coffee shops around the city of Calgary, as we both enjoy the variety of today's coffee beverages and the novelty of discovering quaint, off-the-wall places to drink them in. One day, just prior to picking my friend up for our weekly coffee, I popped by the public library to take out a dozen or so books on the spirit world in my quest to learn more about the supernatural. I no longer had any fear of these books as I did previously, and I felt there was nothing wrong with reading them in our home as God certainly knew my intentions were for the right reasons.

This particular day, my friend and I ventured into a coffee shop housed in an older building that was intriguing and attractive in its décor and its chalk written coffee and menu selections. While ordering our drink and lunch at the counter, we discussed a tip jar in front of us that promised if we deposited money into it, we would receive good karma back in return. We mentioned to each other that we didn't believe in karma, and the lady serving us, overhearing our comment, asked us why? We told her we were Christians and that it wasn't a part of our belief system, which lead us into a brief conversation with her where she shared with us how her brother had died the previous year, and that she felt his spirit was with her over the past year at various times. In fact, she told us she felt his spirit in the coffee shop with her right then as we were speaking.

Wanting the leave her a tip for her friendly service on the counter, I decided I'd drop it into the karma jar instead, seeing as there was a possibility that it might get lifted otherwise. After all, even if it was a karma jar, it didn't mean anything because of my beliefs and convictions as a Christian. Wondering to myself why my friend didn't follow suite in tipping as she usually did, and yet thinking nothing more of it at the time, we picked up our freshly brewed coffee and lunch salads, and took a seat by the window where we ate and caught up with each other's lives since our last coffee outing.

Later that day, after dropping my friend off and heading home with my stack of library books, I spent the early evening reading and scanning through them for more possible insight into the paranormal. My husband during the time I was reading, was taking a nap after work in our bedroom, and had his breathing machine on that he uses for sleep apnea he's suffered with for a number of years. While comfortably reading through in the living room, about an hour or so after I'd opened the books to scan through them, my husband came out of our bedroom with a startled look on his face, and asked me if I had taken his breathing mask off? "Why would I do that?" I asked him. It seems his mask was pulled off his face for some reason and he wasn't sure how it had happened. I figured maybe he'd taken it off himself in his sleep and wasn't even aware of it. I didn't give it any more thought though until we were awakened by our alarm clock at 3:15 early the next morning. We always had our alarm set for the same wake up time each day, and I remembered from previous experience, that this changing of our alarm clock time would occur when these spirits were still active in our home before their removal.

Being quite upset about the idea that our house could once again be haunted, I returned all of the books the next day to the library and called my friend to see if she had witnessed any strange incidents in her home the previous night, wondering if for some reason a spirit or spirits had followed us to our homes from the coffee shop or something. "No, nothing strange has gone on that I know of," she told me. When I explained to her what had happened the night before, she asked me why I put money in the karma jar at the coffee shop. This was something she told me she would never do because of her Christian convictions. Thinking this must have been the reason for the possible return of a spirit or spirits back into our home, I fasted that day, repented, and attended a prayer meeting at our church that evening for corporate prayer about this issue. I was happy to note that afterwards our home was back to normal, and there were no further unusual incidents.

However, several months later I came across another couple of books at the library on the subject of spirits and demons that I wanted to read, and I pondered as to whether I should take them out. After all, the previous incident was likely due to my tipping the karma jar, and probably had nothing to do with my reading about the demonic in our home.

Well, sure enough, I brought these books into our home, all two of them, and began to read them through in our living room, sitting comfortably again on our couch. While I was reading, my daughter decided to cook some perogies for supper for herself (a Ukrainian dumpling that is very popular in our province), and she began to fry them on our stove with some onions and butter. While they were sizzling away in the frying pan, she made a quick run downstairs to grab something, and upon heading back upstairs to the kitchen, she noticed that the stove had been turned off. "Why did you turn the heat off the perogies, Mom?" she asked. "Oh, oh," I thought. "Here we go again!"

Immediately I called a close friend of mine to have her pray for me about this latest incident, and then I proceeded to drive over to the library to drop the books off. While I was at it, I took a number of other books back with me too that were close to overdue, and after depositing all of them in the drop chute, I went into a nearby convenience store to pick up a beverage to drink on the drive home, still questioning God if it was actually the books or something else that was opening the door to the spirits being in our home once more. You can imagine my shock and amazement when I got back into the driver's seat of the truck, to find the two books on ghosts and spirits sitting on the passenger side of the vehicle on the seat! This was the Lord's way of confirming to me that the recent problems in our home were a direct result of my bringing these books under our roof. I quickly took them and re-deposited them in the drop chute, repented, and then fasted once more for deliverance.

Happily, that was the end of the problem once and for all. Now, if I'm interested in reading any books on these topics, I read them in our library, where they stay. What the Lord has taught me through these incidents is that if His Word tells us not to do something, then we had better listen, take heed, and not do whatever it is, whether we believe our intentions are right or not. If the Bible tells us not to do it, *don't do it, even if you think you can justify it!*

"And you shall not bring an abominable thing into your house, and become accursed like it; you shall utterly detest and abhor it; for it is an accursed thing." — Deuteronomy 7:26 RSV

16

Secular Writings on the Paranormal

The writings on the occult are not very often seen in the Christian marketplace, so as a result, I turned mostly to the secular book market to read about other people's experiences with ghosts and the supernatural in general, and to gain their perspectives on this subject outside of the church.

Many experts over the years have tried to disprove the claims of these paranormal activities, and often cling to a few cases that are obviously frauds, or they'll fall back on the statement of the occurrences being *a coincidence*. For those who are still skeptics on the validity of the workings of the spirit realm, Christian or otherwise, I've read numerous accounts of unbelievers that invested their time and money in the attempt to expose paranormal activity as fraudulent, who later emerged from their experiences both surprised and baffled, stating that something is out there that they can't explain away!

A well known Canadian writer by the name of Joe Fisher gave the reader a more personal perspective on the subject of the spirit realm as a former reporter and feature writer for the Toronto Sun and the Toronto Star. He wrote a book back in 1990 called *Hungry Ghosts* and more recently published an update to it entitled, *The Siren Call of Hungry Ghosts, a Riveting Investigation into Channeling and Spirit Guides.*

Previously involved in channeling as outlined in *Hungry Ghosts*, what started out as professional curiosity on his part, ended up becoming an all-encompassing passion of his life as he was won over by the spirits subtle manipulation that came across as great wisdom and love. However, being an investigative journalist by nature, he looked for tangible evidences of these past lives that he obtained through his channeling experiences, only to have his belief system turned upside down, leaving him mentally, physically, and emotionally shaken.

In his book that followed, *The Siren Call of Hungry Ghosts, a Riveting Investigation into Channeling and Spirit Guides,* he tells of how subtle these communicating spirits can be in pulling a person into the wonderful feelings of love and well-being that hooks them totally at the start, and then how slowly, subtly, their manipulation begins in the area of psychological warfare, making it difficult to fight these spirits when they know their victims strengths and weaknesses from the inside out. They are also masters of deception with limited powers of fore-knowledge of past, present and future information that also helps them to impersonate whomever they please with ease, whether the person is dead or alive.

I was shocked and saddened when I looked into obtaining permission from the publishers of Joe's books to quote him, that Joe had committed suicide in 2001. His publisher, Paraview Press, stated that Joe Fisher took his own life on May 9th, 2001 because he was troubled by personal problems and by the spirits he believed he had angered in writing his last book, *The Siren Call of Hungry Ghosts.*

17

———◆———

Three True Stories of
the "New Age Movement"
Dangers

The following are three true stories I'd like to share with you that uncover the dangers involved in dabbling with the occult, even on a seemingly innocent basis. The first is of my great uncle's death predicted by a tarot card reader, the second is of an experience of an acquaintance involving a consultation with a fortune teller, and the third, which I believe to be the most disturbing, was the attempt of an individual to place a curse on a close friend of mine.

These experiences confirm why the Bible warns us to avoid these practices, and also stresses the importance of being baptized under the redeeming blood of Jesus Christ.

As family history goes, many years back in the late 1960's, my great uncle Clarence and his wife Birdie traveled to the province of British Columbia for a short holiday. While in Vancouver, they came across a tarot card reader in the downtown area, and decided for fun to have their cards read by him. To their amazement, this man was able to tell both of them about their pasts, what they did for a living, and what was happening now in their lives. While this was all wonderful and thrilling for them, the thrill soon turned to shock when this fellow, having a spirit of precognition, shared the year and date of my great uncle's death!

After this incident, they vowed they would never again consult anyone practicing the occult, but their vow was soon to be forgotten when my great uncles brother Art, accompanied them a few years later on another trip to Vancouver.

Having heard of Birdie and Clarence's experience with this partic-ular man, Art decided he wanted to have his tarot cards read by him as well. Even with the discouragement of his brother and sister-in-law, he somehow coaxed them into taking him to see this man, and when Clarence refused to accompany him for his reading for obvious reasons, Art not only talked Birdie into going with him, but also into having a reading done for herself too.

Art went for his reading first, and was fascinated at what this man could tell him about his past and present with uncanny accuracy. Curious as to what the future held in store for him, when he questioned the tarot card reader about it, he would not, or could not tell him anything. When he pressured him for an answer, obviously with some concern, all this man would tell him is that he should be very careful traveling through the mountains that day as there was a black cloud over him. As you can imagine, this was extremely upsetting. Not only did this reader not predict his future for him, how did he know they were heading home to Alberta that same afternoon!

To add to the terror and fear Art was experiencing, when Birdie had her cards read next, she was told there was going to be an accident, but that she shouldn't worry because she was going to be ok! With Art not being assured of a future, the mention of a black cloud being over him, and an upcoming accident in Birdie's future, they were terribly upset. And, as Clarence and Birdie would soon find out, this seemingly innocent visit to a tarot card reader would be one of the greatest regrets of their lives.

Due to time commitments, the three of them had to begin their trip back home that same day, and having made it safely as far as Radium Hot Springs in the mountains, they decided to spend the night rather than driving straight through to Alberta. The next morning, with nothing bad happening to them as the tarot card reader had predicted, they felt a whole lot better about things, and had themselves a good breakfast at the motel where they'd stayed before heading out on the road again back to Alberta. However, circumstances were soon to prove tragic.

Shortly after heading out of Radium, they spotted a bear being fed by motorists across the highway, and at the urging of Art, they pulled over to the side of the road to get a better look at the bear and to take some photographs of it. According to my great aunt Birdie, Art was so anxious to see the bear that he was practically out of the car before it stopped moving. While Clarence was loading the film in the camera, Art crossed the road and approached the car on the driver's side of the vehicle, where a woman was feeding the bear through an open window on the passenger side. As he walked to the rear of the car to get a closer look at the bear, the bear suddenly charged towards him, and as Clarence and Birdie looked on, he backed up onto the highway. It was then that Art, and the bear, were hit by a passing vehicle traveling at high speed. Art died instantly on impact, and the bear survived, walking slowly back into the woods.

Uncle Art and myself on our shared birthday

Man killed as he flees bear

A Lethbridge man and a black bear were struck simultaneously by a car in Kootenay National Park Friday.

The man, Arthur Augus Schmitt, 60, was killed, but th· bear got up and walked away.

RCMP at Radium Hot Springs B.C. said the accident occured when Schmitt, accompanied by Mr. and Mrs. Clarence Schmitt, stopped to photograph the bear along Highway 93 near Vermilion Crossing, about 45 miles north of Radium.

While Clarence was still loading his camera, Arthur walked down to see the bear, and as the bear started to move toward him, Arthur backed away into the south-bound traffic lane.

He was struck by a California car driven by Eno Sattler, and the bear, immediately behind him, was also hit.

Great Aunt Birdie and Great Uncle Clarence with my daughter and myself

Over the years since his brother's tragic death, my great uncle Clarence always kept in mind the date that was given him of his appointed death by this man. When the date and time drew near, he expressed his concern to me and several other family members, and was very worried. Back then at that point of time in my life, I was looking for supernatural healing of my MS, and was attending a Bible study group at a local church, still having no true understanding of God and Jesus Christ. However, I did ask this group to pray about my great uncles situation, and they prayed that Jesus would intervene on his behalf. I wrote and told him about the group praying for him, and sure enough, the date of his death came and went, and he ended up living many more years— well into his late 90s in fact.

I believe through corporate prayer, God, through the Lord Jesus Christ, broke the verbal curse that had been placed on him so many years previously.

This second story was told to us by one of the participants in our Bible study group. It involved her former boy friend's visit with a fortune teller, and again, this demonstrates how what is spoken by these people can negatively impact a person's life, even if it doesn't materialize.

A lady from our Bible study group told us about the time she was engaged to a fellow, and after she had broken their engagement for whatever reason, he went to a fortune teller to have his future read. I should mention that at the time of his visit to the fortune teller, this woman had met and fallen in love with another man she had married.

Out of spite I suppose, this former fiancé called her to let her know what had transpired during his visit, and shared with her that the fortune teller told him she was going to have two children with her husband, but that after their second child was born, she was going to come back to him because they were meant to be together.

Our friend told us that she was terrified for years that her husband would die after the birth of their second child, because she knew in her heart she would never leave him. She lived with this fear until their third child was born.

What was spoken to her was a verbal curse, and while her ex-fiancé may not have even believed it, by telling her about it he brought fear into her life that she would not have had otherwise.

"*Death and life are in the power of the tongue.*" — *Proverbs 18:21 KJV*

"*Keep your tongue from evil, and your lips from speaking deceit.*"
— *Psalms 34: 13 RSV*

And last, but not least, is the third true story of the experience a close friend of mine had back in high school, where she was new to our city and a new face at our senior high school.

About 40 years ago, my friend Irene moved to our city from California with her family, to be closer to relatives on her mother's side that lived in southern Alberta.

Irene came from a very strong Pentecostal background and her father was a pastor in that denomination in the United States for a number of years before moving to Canada. Her entire family was very devoted to following Jesus Christ, and they still are today.

I met Irene at high school, and we became good friends at the time, and while I was not a Christian, she and her family were quick to embrace me and I always felt welcomed and loved whenever I visited her home. It was some time later when I got to know her better and was familiar with the faith of Christianity, that Irene shared this story with me of what happened at our high school when she was still a new face in the crowd.

Irene had been studying in our school library, unaware at the time that there was a young student close by who was consulting her spirit guide about a particular homework assignment that needed doing. This girl was an excellent student, and later Irene was to find out that she credited her spirit guide for helping her to achieve the good grades she was receiving. While working on her studies, this guide told this student that she could put a curse on anyone in the library of her choosing, and to just point the person out, and it would go over to them and deliver it. Looking around the room, she spotted Irene's unfamiliar face, and told the guide that she was to be the recipient of the curse that they conjured up together.

As Irene worked away, unknown to her this spirit guide came up to her, and according to the girl, turned around and quickly scurried back. When the girl questioned her guide if it had placed the curse on Irene, it would not give her an answer. After pressuring it though, it finally told her it hadn't, and when she asked it why it hadn't done it, it told her it couldn't because she was *under the blood*. "What's under the blood?" she asked, and surprisingly, it wouldn't answer her. After prodding her guide to no avail, frustrated, she got up and went over to Irene, sat down and introduced herself, and then proceeded to ask her if she knew what under the blood meant. Thinking this was a pretty odd way to get acquainted, Irene explained to her that it meant that you were under the protective blood of Jesus Christ.

It was then that this girl opened up to her and told her about her spirit guide and what had transpired when they tried to place a curse on her. Irene was not only shocked, but told me that she couldn't stop shaking for a long time afterward. However, this incident did open up the opportunity for Irene to share her belief in Jesus Christ with this young student.

Irene writes of this experience: "*It strengthened my faith and confirmed to me that all I had been taught about the Bible was true.*"

"*Ye are of God, little children, and have overcome them: because greater is he that is in you, than he that is in the world.*" — 1 John 4: 4 KJV

Below are several scriptures that explain more in the area of curses, and why we are protected from them as believers through the blood of Jesus Christ.

"*A curse that is causeless does not alight.*" — Proverbs 26: 2 RSV

"*Christ redeemed us from the curse of the law, having become a curse for us.*" — Galatians 3:13 RSV

"*Having cancelled the bond which stood against us with its legal demands; this he set aside, nailing it to the cross. He disarmed the principali-*

ties and powers and made a public example of them, triumphing over them in him." — *Colossians 2:14 RSV*

The Bible also warns us that many common curses are self-imposed. Because of this, you should never entertain bad thoughts or speak them out. Listed in *Deuteronomy 27: 15 – 26,* are a number of other ways curses are received.

18

Human Hypocrisy

According to the dictionary, the definition of hypocrisy is *'feigning to be what one is not or to believe what one does not, or is the false assumption of an appearance of virtue or religion.'* Because personal integrity is what holds our way of life together, young people today are at a loss for life's meaning when they look to mentors that are older and more mature than themselves lacking in integrity, honesty, and truthfulness. And worse yet, how many Christians do they know who profess 'family values' for example, but yet rent x-rated movies and videos, divorce their spouses, and abuse their children at about the same rate as everybody else in society? Where the church used to be different from the world, pointing out the dark side of human nature through the reading of the Epistles of the New Testament to their congregations, many churches today do not confront our carnal nature, believing that tolerance is love and not understanding that tolerance is an impossible virtue when there are no standards.

Being non-judgmental of others is scriptural, but *tolerance without justice* is not because it doesn't help us to face reality through understanding what the negative effects our sin has on us and those around us. Only when we see our shortcomings clearly can we avoid many of the pitfalls in life and understand why we all need a savior.

Sin is defined as *wrongdoing or boundary crossing* from selfishness
    and greed;
Wrongdoing unchecked from selfishness and greed is *tolerance;*
Tolerance of wrongdoing is *indifference;*
Indifference of wrongdoing is *lawlessness;*
Lawlessness is *boundary crossing with no repercussions.*
"Everyone who commits sin is guilty of lawlessness; sin is lawless-
    ness." — 1 John 3: 4 RSV

What many Christians seem to misunderstand about the laws of
the Old Testament and the law of grace in the New Testament, is that
the Old Testament was living by rules, whereas the New Testament
teaching is living by the principles of having a pure heart – a principle
being a truth that is a foundation for all other truths, and is a rule of
action and conduct of uprightness that is achieved through the dying
of 'self' so we can fully love others and ourselves. Never was the law of
grace meant to be a green light for wrongdoing.

*"Behold, the days are coming, says the Lord, when I will make a new
covenant with the house of Judah, not like the covenant which I made with
their fathers when I took them by the hand to bring them out of the land of
Egypt, my covenant which they broke, though I was their husband, says the
Lord. But this is the covenant which I will make with the house of Israel after
those days, says the Lord: I will put my law within them, and I will write it
upon their hearts; and I will be their God, and they shall be my people...
for I will forgive their iniquity, and I will remember their sin no more."*
— *Jeremiah 31: 31 - 34 RSV*

Due to this misunderstanding of the law of grace, many Christians
today often stand in the way of people getting to know the Lord Jesus
Christ by being stumbling blocks, living lifestyles contrary to the Bible's
teachings. What the difference is between this type of Christian and the
informed believer, is that when we sin, we don't say, 'Oh well' and use it
as an excuse to continue in it. We agree with God that it is sin, and we
turn from it and continue on with the new plan of uprightness, asking
for forgiveness, forgiving others and forgiving ourselves. Just as children
learning to walk, we may stumble and fall, but we keep getting up and

pressing on. Unfortunately though, we tend to judge ourselves by our intentions and yet we judge others by their actions. We are lenient with ourselves, but not of others, and this is what Jesus wants us to change about ourselves.

"If you take away from the midst of you the yoke, the pointing of the finger, and speaking wickedness, if you pour yourself out for the hungry and satisfy the desire of the afflicted, then shall your light rise in the darkness and your gloom be as the noon-day. And the Lord will guide you continually and satisfy your desire with good things." — Isaiah 58: 9, 11 RSV

We are all hypocrites in transition it seems, in one way or another, and it is because of this hypocrisy that there are many people who have been wounded by Christian believers, which makes the New Age Movement all the more appealing to them. These are well meaning people, frustrated with Christianity and what it represents or misrepresents, according to what their experience or understanding of it has been. We also seem to forget that it wasn't the Palestine sinners who called for Jesus death on the cross, but the rich, the powerful, and the religious. Jesus attracted immoral outcasts and he came for the sinners of this world, and not for those who arrogantly consider themselves righteous and above correction. The God of the Bible is not a condemning Father, but a Father who loves us enough to teach us about our fallen nature, and how to protect ourselves from the dangers and snares of this world by warning us about what they are, and showing us that above all, we are our biggest problem.

Heresies and immorality will always be in the church with new and old believers alike because all churches are filled with imperfect people, and with people, there will always be problems. However, it is honesty and not perfection that leads us to turn from our wrong doing.

We also need to remember that it is each of us individually who will be facing judgment, and not the particular church we attend, right or wrong, as the mandate of the Bible is that it is ourselves we must change for the better because we all affect one another for the good and the bad. As well, we need the support of the body of believers to become grounded, and by church hopping, hoping to find the perfect church, we set ourselves up for disappointment, resulting in us not having a solid foundation to stand on, learn from, or be a contributing part of. It's been said that once we find a perfect church, it won't be when we attend it, and this is because we are all imperfect.

And as far as different denominations go, Matthew Henry's commentary in his writings in the year 1721 explains this so well: "*Christ is All in all, not here or there, but meets his people with a blessing in every place where he records his name. No party or persuasion has a monopoly on Christ and Christianity.*" Page 348, Volume V Matthew to John

As well, if we find ourselves telling others that our church is the only right one to attend, remember the following verse from the book of Corinthians:

"*Now there are diversities of gifts, but the same Spirit. And there are differences of administrations, but the same Lord. And there are diversities of operations, but it is the same God which worketh all in all.*" — *1 Corinthians 12: 4 – 6 KJV*

19

Spiritual Warfare in the Church

Hypocrisy aside, getting back to the spiritual warfare area of the church, we now have a new generation accepting of witchcraft and wizardry through the *Harry Potter* series, along with other occult influences that appeal to our need for control. With the huge interest this has sparked in children and adults in this area, churches are going to be confronted by problems associated with these practices on an ever increasing scale.

As believers in Jesus Christ, if we are not taught spiritual warfare and the requirements needed to exercise authority in the spirit realm through Jesus Christ, we are of no value to our world in these very anti-Christian times, and for good reason. Pastors, elders, leaders and believers in the church need to know that the time to begin spiritual warfare is not tomorrow, it is today.

"And these signs will follow those who believe; in my name they will cast out demons." — *Mark 16: 17 KJV*

"And ye are complete in Him, which is the head of all principality and power." — *Colossians 2: 10 KJV*

"And gave them power and authority over all devils, and to cure diseases."
— *Luke 9: 1 KJV*

"Behold, I give unto you power to tread on serpents and scorpions, and over all the power of the enemy: and nothing shall by any means hurt you. Notwithstanding in this rejoice not, that the spirits are subject unto you; but rather rejoice, because your names are written in heaven." – Luke 10: 19, 20 KJV

20

Deliverance Prayer and Healing

Just as Simon the Sorcerer believed and was baptized, but yet remained impure in the heart because true repentance had not been made (Acts 8: 13), there are many in the churches that are believers who are also in need of deliverance prayer. As a Christian we might be oppressed if we have bazaar thoughts often, continuing bad dreams, compulsions, or other things that are not normal in behavior or thought patterns. This is not to be confused with those individuals who believe they are experiencing an attack from the devil whenever anything unpleasant happens to them, as it seems in many cases, it is actually the principle of merely reaping what they have sown. It can be backlash received from scorn or disrespect towards others, or even their actions that are contrary to God's Word in the form of lying, stealing, cheating, having a poor work ethic, etc.

When it comes to Deliverance Ministries though, we must return to the Biblical and practical model for spiritual warfare that is centered on discipleship and spiritual discipline, and away from the contemporary, shallow craze of deliverance and exorcism.

"The work of Satan is displayed in all kinds of counterfeit miracles, signs and wonders and in every sort of evil that deceives those who are perishing."
— *2 Thessalonians 2: 9, 10 KJV*

To be a part of a deliverance team that counsels and prays on other people's behalf for oppression, health issues, etc., we must be living righteously, reading the Word of God, and have a consistent life of prayer to be effective. As well, we cannot be involved in any occult practices, having renounced them (*2 Corinthians 4:2*), and we must not have any of the items or books of that nature in our homes or otherwise we will have little or no authority in the spirit realm. Also, those who practice deliverance ministry should be members of a deliverance ministry team as a protective measure and for accountability sake; otherwise all sorts of problems can arise. And to those Christians who believe that casting out evil spirits and praying for the sick and other people's needs is beyond them, remember that it is a practice we are to do as followers of the Lord Jesus Christ.

On the deliverance front, the person receiving deliverance prayer must receive Jesus Christ as their personal savior, or attempts to help them will often have a futile outcome, as witnessed in the 'bad angel' chapter of this book. Also, once the prayer has been completed for a person receiving deliverance, they must be handed over to the safekeeping of God and to a life of living His righteousness.

Physical healing

Interestingly, much of Jesus healing ministry pertained to the breaking of the curses passed down to us from the breaking of the 2nd Commandment.

"You shall not make for yourself an idol… for I, the Lord your God, am a jealous God, visiting the iniquity of the fathers on the children, on the third and the fourth generations of those who hate Me, but show loving-kindness to thousands, to those who love Me and keep My commandments." — *Exodus 20: 4, 5 KJV*

Most Christians have overlooked the curse imposed by breaking this 2nd Commandment that affects our children and future grandchildren, and even our great-grandchildren. We see this all of the time with alcoholism, suicide, obesity, adultery, homosexuality (this could be why some men and women feel they are born this way), divorce, etc. It seems to be ingrained in our physical or psychological makeup for some reason to repeat these sins almost subconsciously, unless we are aware of them and purposely turn away from them. Unfortunately, they can be carried on because we all lead our future generations by example, good or bad. This is why the Bible tells us to inquire of past generations so that we won't be repeating their sins and passing them on (Job 8: 8 KJV). Some of these curses are even in the form of diseases, mental illnesses, deformities, and handicaps, along with violent tempers, self-loathing, etc., and fortunately, as many Christians worldwide have witnessed, God is the same yesterday, today and forever, and He is still in the healing ministry as many have been healed from all these curses and returned to wholeness.

How Forgiveness Brings Healing

An example of a physical healing that happened to me personally came from confronting a woman who was overstepping my boundaries. I had been suffering with discomfort in my chest pretty steady for about a year's time and with having the disease of MS that can cause heart problems; I assumed that this was why I was experiencing this pain. Being someone who doesn't care to see doctors, even at the worst of times, I was putting off seeing one because I felt they could not help me anyway with what I had, especially if it was MS related. What was totally surprising to me was that when I finally got up the nerve to confront this person about past and present issues where she had overstepped with gossip, and forgiving her in the process, the discomfort disappeared overnight. At the time of this writing, it has been over an eight-year period now since I finally got my feelings off my chest, and I've never experienced this pain since. This is where healing can also come into our lives. I would never have guessed this persistent pain in my chest was the result of built up resentment. (*Many times unacknowledged anger, resent-*

ment, hostility or tension from fear or anxiety, comes out as an ache, pain or other health issue.)

God's healing is different for each of us and there is no set formula for it. When Jesus healed people, sometimes he forgave them, sometimes he wiped salve on their eyes, sometimes he cast out demons.[†]

---

† I read in the book *Deliverance Prayer* written by Matthew & Dennis Linn, Paulist Press 1981 BV 227.D44 about a Christian woman with a similar situation like mine who also received negative thoughts, and having tried different churches and secular help to no avail, she surprisingly found freedom from them through a prayer of deliverance by another believer. This true follower of God simply used the authority of Jesus Christ, and quietly bound the spirit and commanded it to leave and never return.

21

Answers to Prayer

The following testimonies are answers to prayer in my life in the past and I'm also including one of a friend that I think is quite humorous. These answers to prayer have been encouraging and uplifting for me personally, and I hope they will be uplifting for you too as you read them.

My Parents' Fiftieth Wedding Anniversary

My parents had decided that they didn't want to rent a hall and invite their friends and relatives for the special event of their fiftieth wedding anniversary, and thought it would be nice to just celebrate it with immediate family instead. Their plan was to have professional photographs taken of them with their children and grandchildren, and then for all of us to go out for dinner and have a social time together afterwards.

Two weeks beforehand, as time was running out for the three of us adult children to complete the planning for the celebration, my sister talked with me about getting our parents a nice cake. I'd told her that I would see what I could do about having a cake made in Calgary, and not knowing what to look for in anniversary cakes; I prayed about it, asking God to guide me in finding a bakery that made them, and to prod me with other ideas for their anniversary to make it special. I had been praying daily for months beforehand that their anniversary would be a special and happy day to be remembered.

Some time earlier, my husband and I had seen a cake made of marzipan, and we thought it would be an appropriate type of cake for this occasion. I opened the telephone book, and called the first number I could find for bakeries, and asked them about the possibility of having a marzipan cake made for us. The baker told me that they didn't make marzipan cakes, but they could recommend me to a very good Danish bakery in downtown Calgary that did. I thanked him, but just before I hung up the phone, I asked him if they made anniversary cakes by chance. He told me they did, and explained that they took old wedding photos of the anniversary couple, and transposed them onto their cakes in an edible form. They were the only bakery in Calgary at that time that made them, and we were thrilled at the idea and placed our order with them.

As well, Chocolates by Bernard Callebaut, which are premium specialty chocolates made in Calgary, came to mind, and we bought them a '50th Anniversary' box along with individual gold, two chocolate boxes, as keepsakes for each of our family members. My husband and I wanted to buy my parents a gift from the two of us to commemorate the day too, and at about this point in time, we saw an ad for the Rosebud Theater on TV that advertised their summer play called *Foxfire* that centered on family values and togetherness. We purchased tickets for the play as our gift to them, and we all enjoyed a wonderful afternoon at this famous dinner theatre situated in the beautiful town of Rosebud, about an hour and a half drive outside of Calgary.

The night before the big day, my husband, daughter and I had packed up and headed to Lethbridge with our chocolates, cake, and a dozen roses in the back of the truck. While on the drive down, my husband wanted to map the miles to Alder Flats for a day of fishing on the river with his dad, who was going to be visiting us from Ontario. Making a wrong turn off the highway, we ended up driving miles and miles on back roads with ruts and deep pits at every turn, and we never did find the area that we were looking for. I was just sick about us having placed the anniversary cake in the back of the truck, and was certain it was ruined. However, when we arrived in Lethbridge that night, the cake was still in perfect shape—truly a miracle!

The next morning, several hours before we would have started getting dressed for our booking at the photographers, the photographer's secretary phoned to tell us he was ill and wouldn't be able to make the sitting. My father had to cancel the appointment then, and we figured maybe we could have a sitting at another time when we were all together again. My sister and I were quite relieved though, as my brother had suggested that we split the cost of the pictures between the three of us as a gift to my parents, but at $1,400.00 a sitting, we weren't too happy about the idea with both of us living on very tight budgets. I talked with my brother about the cancellation, and he decided to ask a good friend if he was free to take photos for us that day. He was available, and wonders of wonders, his girlfriend, who was of high rank in the army, had the army's digital camera home that weekend and he was allowed to use it. Digital cameras were very new on the market back then and very expensive, so this was a real blessing for us to be able to have him use it to take our pictures.

My father, having recently retired from helping my brother with his business, had purchased a home computer earlier in the year, so when the photographs were taken with this digital camera, they were already on a floppy disc and could be inserted into the computer for altering, cutting, copying and printing. This was great for our computer savvy father, who was able to send them afterwards to family & friends via the Internet all at no cost!

When we arrived at the research station outside of Lethbridge that is a beautiful spot for pictures because of the trees and flowers, it was an extremely windy day as it is most days in southern Alberta. As we selected a spot for posing for our first photographs, the wind died down to nothing and did not resume again until about an hour later as our last picture was taken, and we were walking back to our vehicles.

Afterwards, we went out for dinner at a lovely restaurant, and everything about the meal and service was wonderful. We proceeded to my brothers afterwards where we had the cake set out for cutting that was amazing to see with the edible wedding photograph on it of my parents wedding day fifty years earlier. We had it surrounded with a beautiful display of flowers sent by relatives and friends, lit candles, and the chocolates displayed in their golden boxes. My brother had also gone through my parents old photo slides weeks earlier, and supplied the entertainment for the evening by giving us a slide show of pictures of our family over the years, from childhood up to adulthood. We split the cost of everything between the three of us, so it was done with very little damage to our pocketbooks.

It was a beautiful, perfect anniversary day in every detail, and everyone was saying that it was like everything was meant to be. And, to top it all off, even the photograph of my parents that was put in the newspaper afterwards announcing their anniversary, was so unusual and beautiful, that people were calling to ask who the photographer was! I'm still thrilled when I think about it.

Wilf's Funeral

Having had such a good experience after inviting God into my parent's fiftieth wedding anniversary, while a funeral is not the cause for celebration but of much sorrow, I decided to have our prayer group at the church I attended, pray with me that we would know and experience God's presence at his memorial service on the Friday of the coming week.

Wilf was the father of my brother-in-law, and over a twenty-year time period, we had all gotten to know and love him. He was a strong member of the Anglican Church in Medicine Hat and Lethbridge, and was always volunteering in the community, helping wherever he could. He even received the Volunteer of the Year award from the City of Medicine Hat the year of his death, and this was when he was 80 years of age. He is a good reminder to all of us that age has no limits when it comes to our capacity to give of ourselves.

Along with being very involved with his church and community, he also was an active member of the Nanton Lancaster Society Museum in Nanton, Alberta. Wilf was a tail gunner in the war in the Lancaster aircraft, and was one of the few airmen to survive such a vulnerable position of attack. For all the years we had known him, he had attended every air show in Lethbridge, bringing his four boys with him from the time they were youngsters to this yearly event. He was very proud to have served his country, and he enjoyed the opportunity each year to see many of these great planes once more in the skies.

The day of his memorial service, family and friends, along with his fellow comrades from the air force, gathered together at the grave site while his Pastor shared memories and laughter about Wilf and his enjoyment of life. At the conclusion of the service, the Taps began to play, and salutes from fellow air force comrades from the war were given him. It was very beautiful and yet so incredibly sad. However, just at the moment that the service ended, and we were about to turn to leave the grave site, there was a fly over of five jets above us, their noise shocking us, and causing us to look up in awe. The attendant at the funeral made the comment that the fly over couldn't have been better choreographed if they had planned it! It was the perfect ending of a lovely farewell to someone who loved his air planes, life, and the air force so much.

Afterwards, everyone went to my mother's home for refreshments, and because of the heat of the summer, she had set up the tables with food and drinks outside on the driveway under the carport where it was considerably cooler. What happened next was even more evidence that God was present.

After we had all arrived and took our seats at the outdoor luncheon, war planes began flying overhead. The annual air show was scheduled for that particular weekend in Lethbridge, and the planes taking part in it were flying in from all over the world to participate. To our amazement, as we all stood up to watch, shortly after the planes flew overhead, sky divers with their red smoke billowing from their ankles, descended in front of us in a field a short distance away. Wilf's sons discussed amongst themselves, having been to every air show over the years, that it was unusual that the sky divers were practicing their landings in that particular field, seeing as all of the years previously they had watched them land at a school ground in the center of the city.

I don't believe any of this was a coincidence and I believe this was God's way of showing us that His presence was with us. Nobody does things better than God when we ask.

Saving through Grace

This incident I'm about to tell you happened about ten years ago when I was listening to an old Bible study tape on the book of Daniel, taught by Charles R. Swindoll back in 1976. The tapes were called *Insight for Living – Daniel – God's Pattern for the Future* and the particular tape I was listening to was on the book of Daniel, chapter six.

About mid-way through the tape on the lesson, Charles speaks of the King's sleepless night in Daniel 6:18, and as he talks about the anguish of it, he tells the listener of a situation with a women at his church who had lost her sister in a motor vehicle accident, and how she could not get over the loss and was in continual anguish over it. Thinking at the time of how much my own sister meant to me, immediately it was brought to my mind that my sister and her husband were traveling just then to Calgary to pick up their daughter from the airport. Realizing that I'd forgotten to pray for their safety, I stopped the tape and prayed on their behalf, thanking God that I could give my worries to Him and experience wonderful peace as a result. As I turned the tape back on again and was about to continue with the lesson (this man is a fabulous teacher), the telephone rang, and it was my mother calling to chat and to tell me that I should be watching a particular TV program she was enjoying. We talked for all of 10 minutes and immediately after we hung up, the telephone rang again, and this time it was my brother-in-law calling from a payphone on the side of the road outside of a small town on the way to Calgary. They had hit a very large deer on the highway and their vehicle was totaled, so they needed me to pick their daughter up at the airport for them, seeing as we were still lived in Calgary at the time. When I asked him what time the accident happened, he told me, "Oh, about 10 minutes ago." I was so shocked that I blurted out to him that I had been praying for their safety just 10 minutes earlier!

Fortunately for them, this accident happened close to a service station just outside of this small town, and they were able to use its outdoor pay phone to call the Alberta Motor Association for a tow truck, one of which was heading on its way back from Calgary to Lethbridge. This was why they were able to call us almost immediately afterwards and why they had no problem getting back home with the AMA truck driver there to tow them. Can you believe God would use a Charles Swindoll Bible study tape on the book of Daniel made back in 1976 to prompt me to pray for my sister and brother-in-law's safety? I do.

"Gift for Obedience"

In recent years, because of my better understanding of scripture and how offended God is when we practice anything that is pagan in origin, the hypnosis incident being a clear indication to me, I decided to discontinue my practice of buying lotto tickets and scratch and win's for my husband and family members for their birthdays. This was because of the addictive spirit behind them that can develop into a stronghold in a person's life, and the fact that I had never believed in luck anyway, even though to this day I still find myself using the term *luck* without thinking, it is so ingrained into our language and thinking.

On top of this sudden insight, I began to realize how superstitious I was when I came across a plastic container with a black lid on it that was on sale for a great price. Our daughter needed some storage boxes in her room, but I could not bring myself to buy this container because of the color of the lid. To me it meant something bad might happen if I bought it. After picking it up and returning it several times back to its shelf in the store, I decided that it really wasn't right to be thinking like that, so I went ahead and bought it anyway.

The next morning, my husband and I were watching the tail end of a Christian program on television, and the guest on the show, who was very knowledgeable in scripture, was discussing how using the word *luck* was wrong, and how *superstition* was not of God either. I was surprised to hear this and was thankful that I never believed in luck, and that I had fought the urge to be superstitious the night before.

As soon as the program had ended, I received a phone call from our bank bearing good news. When I had made a donation to the charity organization called the United Way at our bank branch some weeks earlier, they had put my name in for a draw for one of two wicker baskets loaded with goodies. They had just drawn my name, and I was the winner of the larger of the two baskets!

What was the real surprise for me about winning this beautiful wicker basket with all of the wonderful treats and items inside was that it contained a gift certificate to the Keg, a steak restaurant that is very popular here in Canada. This was very special to me because I could never get my husband to take me there. He wouldn't take me no matter how often I'd asked over our then '18 years' of marriage, and this was probably because he was a hunter and we always had good meat in our freezer. But now there was no excuse! We used the certificate and had not only an excellent meal, but a wonderful time out together too.

Could this have been a coincidence? Not for me. Because the God of the Bible is a personal God, I took this as an affirmation from Him that what I was choosing to do was right according to His Word.

Sukkoth

A number of years ago, our small group leader introduced us to studying the Old Testament and as a result, we became fascinated with its history, studying Daniel and the books of Ezra, Esther and Nehemiah, and The Feasts of Israel. Then my nephew gave me a Hebrew calendar for Christmas the following year that outlined *The Feasts of Israel* that are celebrated during the various months of the Jewish calendar year. As a result, as a small group we celebrated *Purim,* taken from the book of Esther (9:20 – 22), and even had a *Seder Plate for Passover* (telling the Haggada, which is the story of the Exodus in the Bible). The Jewish calendar months are different than ours, so without a Jewish calendar, it would have been difficult for us to acknowledge the feasts at the same time of year as the Jews do. Fascinated by it all, we celebrated *Hanukkah* (the celebration of the rededication of the temple at Jerusalem back in 165 B.C.) with our family, and even baked their traditional braided bread for the *Shabbat* (the Jewish Sabbath) several times, the Shabbat being similar to our equivalent of Sunday in Western culture. As well, we celebrated the Biblically ordained holidays of *Rosh Hashanah* (the Jewish New Year), and *Yom Kippur* (the High Holiday of public and private atonement to become right with God and others), where I had the opportunity to attend a synagogue for the first time.

However, with the up and coming festival of the *Sukkoth* (the feast of booths in Leviticus 23: 33 – 44), I had no idea how a person could celebrate it, seeing as it commemorated the temporary shelters used by the Jews during their wandering in the wilderness. This was one festival I would have to miss, and yet looking back over the past year, I marveled at how blessed I'd been personally with each of the celebrations of these Feasts of Israel. I highly recommend celebrating these festivals not only as learning tools of the Jewish culture and because there's great food involved, but because I do believe it pleases God who chose the Jews to give the doctrine of our faith to humanity through.

Getting back to the *Sukkoth* though, I'd completely forgotten about it when a friend of mine called me to ask if I would like to come up to visit her at her time share in Panorama, B.C. for a week. I had other commitments until mid-week and then I drove up on the Wednesday afternoon to meet her there. To my surprise, in Panorama, B.C., located at the top of a mountain, there are no shopping malls or restaurants, just nature trails to walk, horseback riding and golfing, and an outdoor hot tub and swimming pool, coffee shop and small grocery store. My friend cooked us a delicious supper that evening that was followed by the opportunity for me to look at photographs she had taken when she visited Israel earlier that year. The next day we walked on nature trails, and enjoyed the beauty of the outdoors and the pools while we visited and relaxed. It was very beautiful and peaceful and was a perfect way to reflect on life and creation. What was the real surprise for me though was when I went to retire the first night of arriving, and having my daily devotional material with me, I turned to the days date on my Jewish calendar to read its caption. To my amazement, it was the eve of the *Sukkoth!* (All Jewish festivals begin the evening before.) There I was in a temporary dwelling, in a place where the visitors time is spent enjoying the outdoors and reflecting on creation. I didn't have to miss celebrating this festival after all!

Angels from God

I had to add this last true story of answered prayer even though it wasn't an answer to my own prayers, but someone else's. This happened to the sister of a lady in our Bible study class, and it demonstrates what a wonderful sense of humor God has too.

One of the ladies in our group had asked for prayer for safety for her sister and brother-in-law who were traveling by motorcycle through the mountains of British Columbia in early spring. When we prayed for them, we asked God to put Angels of protection around them to keep them safe on their holiday. After praying for her sister, this lady said that she could almost see the angels guiding them as they traveled along the highway.

The following week, when this ladies sister had returned from her trip, she had quite the story to tell us. Apparently her sister and her husband got caught in a very bad rain storm as they were ascending one of the Rocky mountains, and wet, shaking and soaked to the bone, they made it to a service station where the attendants took pity on them, and provided them with garbage bags to pull over their heads to cover themselves for warmth, and to protect them from the elements and cold on their descent down the mountain.

Shaken and scared at the idea of heading down the mountain in the storm, they saw a group of bikers, and her sister ran over to them to ask if they could ride down the mountain with them. They welcomed them into their group and not only allowed them to ride with them, but they surrounded them with their motorcycles. They had bikes in front of them as well as bikes positioned at angles beside them and behind them. After making it safely down the mountain, the bikers offered them a place to sleep, but declining, they found the nearest motel to crash as they hit their bed in exhaustion. This may seem farfetched, but could the bikers have been Hells Angels, a notorious motorcycle gang that is prevalent here in Canada and the U.S.? Could these have been the angels that surrounded them that we prayed for? Who knows? God does tell us He will use anyone to accomplish His purposes, and just the idea of it makes this one of the funniest answers to prayer I've ever heard!

"For the eyes of the Lord are over the righteous and his ears are open unto their prayers: but the face of the Lord is against them that do evil." — *1 Peter 3: 12 KJV*

I can't begin to share all of the answers to prayer we've received over the past twelve years as Christians, but I can tell you that it is more than worth the effort to have a consistent prayer life. The ministry of prayer is open to everyone and we are so foolish not to access it. God is a sovereign God who tells us we can move His hand in prayer on our own and others behalf and no prayers are wasted and not heard by God. As a good friend once told me, prayers can accumulate and then the clouds of prayer finally burst and God rains His blessings on us. Never stop praying!

Some Final Thoughts

Because many people have not had the gospel of Jesus Christ explained to them in a way they can respond to, here is a clear explanation of salvation and what being born again means. Keep in mind that salvation is not an event, but it is the beginning of a process for positive change with the help of God's Holy Spirit, given to all believers through the redeeming blood of Jesus Christ.

The word *salvation* means the act of saving or the state of being saved, offering preservation from destruction, ruin, loss or calamity. Salvation through Jesus Christ means not only saving us to eternal life, but helping us to save ourselves from unnecessary harm while we are alive on earth. In order to understand all of this, we need to break down the good and evil that is in our carnal nature, beginning with our flesh and spirit.

Flesh and Spirit

We are *born of the Flesh*, which means we are connected with the appetites and passions of the body. *In the Flesh*, because none of us lives a life where our needs are always being met, we often behave irresponsibly, unrealistically, and irrationally in an unsuccessful attempt at meeting our needs. *Flesh is also referred to as 'ego'* – which is looking at everyone and everything only as it affects us and our own welfare, seeing self as the center of all things.

Spirit however, is different in that it is the immaterial part of man that involves our soul, our beliefs and our emotional being. *In the Spirit, our beliefs and emotions drive how we respond to our fleshly needs and desires; and if the important people in our lives did not know, discuss, or point out right and wrong behavior to help us come out of our self-centeredness, the reality of the negative after effects of our behavior cannot be clearly understood by us.*

The Bible teaches that corruption and sin are woven into our nature and that it is our nature that must be changed. Corrupt nature is *Flesh* and is the 1st birth, and the new nature in Jesus is *Spirit*, that takes rise from the 2nd birth.

"Verily, verily, I say unto thee, except a man be born of water and of the Spirit, he cannot enter into the kingdom of God. That which is born of the flesh is flesh; and that which is born of the Spirit is spirit." — Jesus, John 3: 5, 6 KJV

In Him, we correct our wrongs where we can; we forgive others throughout life and ask them to forgive us; we become fair in our dealings as honesty and truthfulness become a part of our nature; we become promise keepers and develop courage to face difficulties and to stick with what is right even under pain; we begin to use practical common sense that takes the trouble to think out what we are doing and what is likely to come of it; we stop judging others, understanding that only God knows all sides of our lives and the history that has shaped us; we ask ourselves, *what would God* think of our conduct and actions as a husband, wife, parent, grand-parent, step-parent, son, daughter, friend, employer, employee, mentor, pastor, and all other hats we might be wearing, *and what can I do to change for the better.* We understand that when we behave in such a way that we give and receive love with pure motives, feeling worthwhile to ourselves and others, our actions, words, and thoughts become right and moral. Above all, we learn not to become comfortable in our irresponsibility's through understanding that *unless we judge our own behavior and stop justifying ourselves as to why we may be behaving badly, we will not change.*

Life is difficult, and when we don't change our selfish ways, we often make life more burdensome for ourselves and those around us than it should be, as our thoughts, words and actions can be extremely destructive to one another in both our fleshly and spiritual nature. *The heart of Christianity is the changing of ourselves as individuals through Jesus Christ, giving us a social consciousness that extends outside of self and into a genuine love for humanity.*

Flesh is me, myself and I, and revolves around our needs and it is self-centered in its attempt to meet these needs through temporal, materialistic, fleshly, and other worldly means. *Spirit* is caring for the things of the soul that are sacred, which is achieved through loving others, being proactive in helping those in need, and having *the courage to confront all that is wrong in our thinking and actions.* It is maintaining healthy boundaries with ourselves and others, with the Holy Spirit encouraging us through His influence, stirring us up to act rightly towards all of mankind *regardless of our feelings, emotions or physical needs.*

As Christians, we apply our faith continually throughout our lives through self-examination and correction, as the Bible teaches us: *"The heart is deceitful above all things, and desperately wicked: who can know it? I the Lord search the heart; I try the reins, even to give every man according to his ways, and according to the fruit of his doings."* — *Jeremiah 17: 9, 10 KJV*

"For from within, out of the heart of men, proceed evil thoughts, adulteries, fornications, murders, theft, covetousness, wickedness, deceit, lasciviousness, an evil eye, blasphemy, pride, foolishness. All these evil things come from within and defile the man." — *Mark 7: 21 – 23 KJV*

"Keep thy heart with all diligence: for out of it are the issues of life." — *Proverbs 4: 23 KJV*

"Every way of a man is right in his own eyes: but the Lord pondereth the hearts." — *Proverbs 21: 2 KJV*

If we would like to be *Born Again* under the New Covenant as spoken of in *Jeremiah 31: 31 – 34*, it all begins with a simple prayer:

> *"Father, I am a sinner and I ask you to forgive me as I repent of my sinning. (Take a few moments to ask forgiveness for what is on your conscience.) I believe what Your Word tells me about my carnal nature, and I invite you into my heart in the name of Jesus Christ to be born again into Your Spirit nature, receiving Jesus Christ as my personal savior for the remission of my sins, and for a clear conscience."*

With our now purified hearts, *we receive the 'Holy Spirit'* that opens our eyes to love all of humanity with its imperfections and flaws. We begin to see ourselves and others through the eyes of love and through the washing of His Word, we are changed step by step as the healing begins from any trauma in our lives, and strongholds start to fall away as our thinking becomes transformed through the renewing of our minds.

As we begin to view ourselves as the *Saints* that the Lord now sees us as—Jesus in us and working through us—*wrongdoing strangely begins to lose its hold,* and our lives begin to come together for the positive as we live in the Spirit of compassion, kindness, patience, and forgiveness. We put away anger, malice, slander and foul talk from our mouths, and we no longer lie to one another, having put off the old nature (animal nature) and put on the new nature (divine nature). While we will always have shortcomings, our major flaws are done away with and our character is then continually being shaped and developed from the study and application of the Word of God to our lives.

Baptism is the next step, and while God knows our hearts and baptism itself doesn't save us, *we are asked to be baptized under the name of 'Jesus Christ' as done in Acts 2: 38,* because it symbolizes a conscious break in becoming dead to self—being buried to the old nature—and rising up again into the new nature in the unity of the Holy Spirit. It is closing the door on our old life, and opening the door to the new life just as Noah closed the door on the flood waters to new life; the Israelites crossing of the Red Sea had the door of water closed on their old life as they entered their new life; and the male and female united in marriage, who close the door on self to create new life together in unity. Baptism is our public testimony of our merge into the oneness of God's Spirit through Jesus Christ, and it helps to keep us accountable to our brethren by putting a face to us as new family members of the church body. Our faith should not be secret, and if it wasn't important to be baptized in the presence of one or more persons, we could all baptize ourselves, but this is not scriptural.

We must be cautious at this point too, to not be repeating the common mistake of not forsaking the company of unhealthy companions, environments and habits upon salvation, or we will live the up and down experience in our faith of continually slipping and falling that is familiar to the average church member today. Remember as well, that even though we have accepted Jesus Christ as our savior, the world around us hasn't, so our walk with Him may seem futile to begin with. As we change for the better though, the world around us will too, and a lot of peace will come to us when we realize, for example, that God is our father and mother, as this takes the judgment off of our natural parents who are only human, and sinners like the rest of humanity. *Forgiveness,* whether it be for our upbringing, wrongdoing committed against us or loved ones, generational sins, or our own poor choices, *is letting go of all hopes for a better past, and frees us to walk out of it and into a promising future, forgiven and forgiving.*

We need to attend a church that teaches the good and dark side of our human nature; be a part of a ministry that helps the downtrodden; teach all children the time-tested truths of scripture and be positive mentors for them by living out these truths; read the Bible and join a Bible study class; and maintain our relationship in prayer with God through *A.C.T.S.—Adoration, Confession, Thanksgiving, and Supplication.* God heals the brokenhearted and binds up their wounds (Psalm 147: 3 KJV) and will restore us to wholeness as we walk in His Spirit of righteousness and charity.

God through Jesus Christ will give us a hope and a purpose for our lives and it will be as individual as we are.

"And now why tarriest thou? Arise, and be baptized, and wash away thy sins, calling on the name of the Lord." — Acts 22: 16 KJV

Gift Ideas

To your enemy, forgiveness
To an opponent, tolerance
To a friend, your heart
To a customer, service
To all, charity
To every child, a good example
To yourself, respect.

— Oren Arnold

CPSIA information can be obtained at www.ICGtesting.com
Printed in the USA
LVOW102045051011

249268LV00002B/1/P